More Praise for *The Mindful Marketer*

"A unique way of looking at Marketing using the principles of Mindfulness. Making decisions by being present and in the moment can enhance the relevance and growth of your business. This book is a must read."
—Michael Tompkins, CEO, Miraval Resorts

"In today's customer-centric organizations, uncertainty is the new norm. It's time for CMOs and their teams to carve a new path. Lisa's book provides a formula for mindfully managing through uncertainty. Take the first step and read *The Mindful Marketer*!"
—Jamie S. Gorski, CMO, The Bozzuto Group

"While scads of marketing experts out there teach you to do more, Lisa Nirell actually shows you how you can be more. Read Lisa's important new book, and begin your journey to marketing nirvana."
—Mark Levy, Author of *Accidental Genius: Using Writing to Generate Your Best Ideas, Insight, and Content*

This page intentionally left blank

THE MINDFUL MARKETER

How to Stay Present and Profitable in a Data-Driven World

Lisa Nirell

THE MINDFUL MARKETER
Copyright © Lisa Nirell, 2014.

Softcover reprint of the hardcover 1st edition 2014 978-1-137-38629-8

All rights reserved.

First published in 2014 by
PALGRAVE MACMILLAN®
in the United States—a division of St. Martin's Press LLC,
175 Fifth Avenue, New York, NY 10010.

Where this book is distributed in the UK, Europe and the rest of the world, this is by Palgrave Macmillan, a division of Macmillan Publishers Limited, registered in England, company number 785998, of Houndmills, Basingstoke, Hampshire RG21 6XS.

Palgrave Macmillan is the global academic imprint of the above companies and has companies and representatives throughout the world.

Palgrave® and Macmillan® are registered trademarks in the United States, the United Kingdom, Europe and other countries.

ISBN 978-1-349-48156-9   ISBN 978-1-137-38631-1 (eBook)
DOI 10.1057/9781137386311

Library of Congress Cataloging-in-Publication Data

Nirell, Lisa, 1961–
   The mindful marketer : how to stay present and profitable in a
data-driven world / Lisa Nirell.
     pages cm
   Includes bibliographical references.

    1. Branding (Marketing) 2. Strategic planning. 3. Decision making.
I. Title.

HF5415.1255N57 2014
658.8—dc23   2014010223

A catalogue record of the book is available from the British Library.

Design by Newgen Knowledge Works (P) Ltd., Chennai, India.

First edition: September 2014

10 9 8 7 6 5 4 3 2 1

CONTENTS

List of Figures and Tables — ix
My Greatest Fear About This Book — xi
Chris Brogan
Acknowledgments — xiii

SECTION 1

| Chapter 1. | Why CMOs Are Facing Extinction | 3 |

Ten troubling trends provide a unique opportunity for marketing leaders to change course and adapt.

| Chapter 2. | The Dark Side of Data Democracy | 11 |

The Web fosters a level of transparency that we have never seen. Whom can you—and your customers—trust?

| Chapter 3. | Going DIM: Can You See (or Hear) Me Now? | 19 |

The pervasive Digital Intrusion Movement (DIM) tempts us to let technology dictate our every move. What unique, fleeting life experiences are we missing?

| Chapter 4. | Return on Marketing Investments: A Flight Risk? | 25 |

Expanded budget authority does not give marketing leaders license to fly at unsafe speeds. Here are 3 common obstacles.

| Chapter 5. | Big Data or Big Disappointment? | 31 |

Analytics miss half of what customers are saying online. Where is the balance between data and wisdom?

| Chapter 6. | Marketing and Sales: A Hard Landing | 41 |

Three areas create the most friction between sales and marketing: Data, Roles, and Content.

| Chapter 7. | Multitasking Mash-ups and Mishaps | 51 |

Information overload and multitasking erode productivity and quality of life. Here's the research to prove it, and ways to eradicate these habits.

SECTION 2

Chapter 8.	Find Your *Inner Marketing Guru* to Make Better Decisions	61
	Experts encourage marketers to do more. I suggest you need to be more. These seven mindfulness precepts will help.	
Chapter 9.	Western Mindfulness: A Brief Journey	69
	Mindfulness can provide true refuge when we lose our balance and focus. Which practices resonate with you?	
Chapter 10.	Five Timeless Qualities of Mindful Marketers	79
	Acceptance, aliveness, articulateness, aggregation, and adaptability—the traits that help you find your true nature and Inner Marketing Guru.	
Chapter 11.	Personal Energy Management	87
	Personal energy field management is not some New Age pablum. It's what separates exhausted marketing leaders from vibrant ones.	
Chapter 12.	The Power of Present Moment Language	95
	Intentional, empathic leaders know what areas they can and cannot influence. This clarity allows them to communicate and persuade with greater ease.	
Chapter 13.	Mindful Planning and Decision-Making	105
	Mindfulness represents fresh ingredients in our marketing leadership recipe; critical thinking is the Mason jar. Critical thinking fuels career longevity.	
Chapter 14.	Designing with Intention	115
	Ways to incorporate intentionality into our work environments—where innovation often emerges. Subtle design shifts fosters empathy, focus, and productivity.	

SECTION 3

Chapter 15.	Peer Groups: How Shifts *Really* Happen	125
	Do you rely mostly on Klout scores and "likes" to guide your career journey, or on a personal force field of trusted peers?	

CONTENTS

Chapter 16.	What the CEO Wants the CMO to Know	135
	Modern marketers, fluent in content, media, and analytics, often speak Greek. These are three essential qualities to engage with your CEO in plain English.	
Chapter 17.	*CFO-Speak*: Mindful Marketing by the Numbers	145
	CFOs are often a key business partner to the CEO. You need these five steps to attain financial fluency and alignment with your CFO.	
Chapter 18.	The CMO and the CIO: Crossing the Raging River	155
	On the raging river of IT and marketing discontent, it can be tough to find common ground. Here is how to stay afloat and row together.	
Chapter 19.	Sales and Marketing: Rethinking the System	165
	Four strategies to close the gap between sales and marketing, inspired by systems thinking and Martin Luther King.	
Chapter 20.	Looking Inside to Work Outside	175
	Are your leadership approaches consistent with all external stakeholders? Five marketers share strategies to build powerful, mindful external relationships.	
Chapter 21.	Starting the Revolution	185
	What will fuel your mindful marketing revolution? A reference chart to guide customer-centered marketing strategies is included.	
Chapter 22.	Minding the Future	195
	Mindful marketers constantly make room for their true brilliance to shine, and to discover new opportunities. These 6 trends are worth watching.	

About Lisa Nirell	203
Notes	205
Index	219

This page intentionally left blank

FIGURES AND TABLES

FIGURES

1.1	Survey of CMOs	9
1.2	Point 1-Final	9
2.1	The Information Buzz	12
6.1	Sales and Marketing Harmony Formula	42
6.2	Content Engine	47
7.1	Treat Each Task Like a Single Prayer Bead	56
8.1	Your Inner Marketing Guru	63
10.1	Clarity Attention Guide	83
12.1	The Persuasion Pyramid	97
13.1	Performance Accelerant Model	109
14.1	Enlighted's Human-Aware Systems	121
15.1	Customer Advisory Board	127
16.1	The Super CMO Zone	138
16.2	The Three Time Horizons Model	142
17.1	The Customer Experience Measurement Ecosystem Graphic	150
18.1	Which Monk Are You?	156
18.2	Table McKinnon	161
19.1	Service Level Agreement	171
20.1	Was Buddha One of the Early Improv Performers?	179

TABLES

12.1	The Marketing Language Meter	100
17.1	How Does Your Business Stack Up?	153
21.1	Internal vs. External Marketing Approaches	190

This page intentionally left blank

MY GREATEST FEAR ABOUT THIS BOOK

I'm afraid. I'll tell you that outright. As I've read through Lisa's book, I can only come to one realization: the people who need to read this book probably won't. This book is loaded with mindfulness advice, with touchy-feely huggy-squishy advice, the kind that marketers love to delete/ignore/skip over. Let me give you an example.

This young man has been bugging me fairly incessantly for "social media" advice, very specifically, metrics. He keeps asking me for "key performance indicators," as if there's a magical formula. Replace the phrase "social media" with "fax" or "telephone," and you realize how silly the question really is. But more so, the question betrays the larger problem.

We are *dying* for a magical number. "If you send eight emails, make two YouTube videos, and mail an archaic postcard, anyone will buy anything!" I swear to you, my unknown friend, that if I blogged this on my website, people would start putting it on slides and showing it off at marketing meet-ups. (Not that I'm some kind of prophet, but more so that people are still so desperate for a magical number.)

And this is the problem: if you're reading chapter 8, about finding your inner marketing guru, and you're not shuddering while reading it, I'm a little scared in the other direction. That's the thing. I just came up with an easy way to think of it:

Scared is very close to Sacred, at least in spelling.

You'll get a lot of value out of this book, I'm guessing, because you've picked it up. There's a chance you'll read it. If you were drawn here by magical forces, there's a chance you'll give this a go. But the people who need it? Those who are most in jeopardy of becoming machines? Well, do you think they'll give it a try?

So here's the assignment: read this book, love it, do what needs doing, and then secretly hide the best and most important lessons you learn here in other people's "numbers" marketing, their robot machinations.

Be the secret revolution. That's the only way Lisa will be able to spread this kind of message, I suspect.

I'm scared. Or I'm sacred. Either way, it's a heck of a show.

CHRIS BROGAN
publisher *Owner Magazine*

ACKNOWLEDGMENTS

The path to *The Mindful Marketer* started 13 years ago—and I was too afraid to tell anyone in my business community about it. In 1999, I "accidentally" discovered a community of spiritual seekers while I was living in San Diego, California. They forever changed my worldview. Stepping back from the rigors of traditional corporate life helped me understand why some businesses thrive, and others merely exist to turn a profit. This book would have never come to life without that initial spark.

I bow to my global team of business gurus, writing coaches, muses, and philosophers. Each of you plays a key role in fueling my mind, body, and spirit. I extend my heartfelt gratitude to them here:

THE MIND ALCHEMISTS

Greg Clowminzer, my first business coach, who introduced me to a world beyond the corporate walls. He taught me the joy of chaos, compassion, and silence. Greg guided me through some of the most challenging personal times in my adult life and helped me discover my inner entrepreneur.

Alan Weiss, my mentor of seven years. I am honored to know you, and appreciate your showing me how to communicate my message and expertise to the world. You demonstrated that the term "writer's block" is a mirage—now I cannot imagine my life without a pen or keyboard at my disposal at all times! I think bigger because of you.

Mark Levy, my writing coach. Behind your improvisational comedy talent lies an innate ability to bring out the best in creative people. This book would have never seen the light of day without your guidance and encouragement.

John Willig, my agent. You are a true professional who understands the trials and tribulations of the publishing industry. Thank you for believing in this book, and for showing me the classic beauty of Bryant Park.

Here's to the incredible Palgrave publishing team: Laurie Harting, a fellow yogini and editor par excellence. You inspired me to become a better writer and communicator. I will be forever grateful for your painstaking efforts to improve every chapter. Lauren LoPinto, you kept me on track with every publishing milestone and made this process move forward with ease. Rachel Taenzler—Great work during the finals print!

My clients and marketing community members: I don't have enough space here to mention everyone. You collectively helped me launch the first community of like-minded marketing practitioners and mindful leaders. Now, hundreds of CMOs later, we are co-creating models and ways of being that are transforming the marketing profession. I tip my hat to Susan Weber, Jamie Gorski, Philip Lay, Geoffrey Moore, Wendy Lea, Jascha Kaykas-Wolff, Guy Kawasaki, Jen Kern, Greg Jorgensen, David Hassell, Stuart Itkin, Tim Hill, Chip Coyle, and Rob Pinkerton.

To CJ Madigan, my publishing Sherpa. You were an unexpected gift. As we navigated these winter months together and assembled the manuscript, I knew that I could focus on what I do best—researching, distilling, and writing. You kept the process on track. You never disappointed. I am forever grateful to Sarah White for introducing us, and look forward to our next collaboration.

THE "BODY TEAM"

My best ideas emerge when I am wandering outdoors in nature or swimming in open water. Coach Bob Bruce, my spiritual swim coach of five years, inspired me to brave the chilliest Elk Lake waters and reach impossible distance goals. Today, because of Bob, I register for 5K swim races without flinching. I cannot imagine staying balanced and focused without his years of coaching, pool humor, and encouragement.

I also bow to the late Gabrielle Roth, innovator of the *Five Rhythms*® global dance phenomenon. You showed me how movement, creativity, and mindfulness are inextricably linked. Ever since we met at Esalen five years ago, I have seen how music and ecstatic dance are timeless catalysts for refining our intuitive powers, connecting with others, and living life fully.

THE SPIRIT TEAM

My husband Magnus, a recovering atheist, is one of my most important spiritual teachers. In the past three years, Magnus has transformed his

ACKNOWLEDGMENTS

life through community service, outreach, and contemplative study. When I face any ethical or emotional crossroads, you help me find my center again. As we enter our 26th year of marriage, you are my true refuge.

Our cats, Bella and Big B. They reinforce the loving-kindness and humor of Buddha. I cannot imagine life without these little monsters. They are ever present, and ever mindful.

Jonathan Foust, the cofounder of Insight Meditation Community of Washington (IMCW). You welcomed me to Washington, DC, in 2010. Relocating from the West Coast to the East Coast was no easy transition for me. I dove head first into your meditation programs and silent retreats, and watched my new life here blossom. You helped me to find a middle path between making money and making meaning.

My soul sisters (and brother): Diana Cutler, Karen Walker, Lisa McClave, Karen Gallardo, Kirsti Lindberg-Repo, Cathy Hawk, Chuck Everhart, and Angela Heilbrunn. How can I ever thank you for your friendship, laughter, and encouragement? You traveled hundreds—sometimes thousands—of miles to meet me, hear my tales of transition, and share our mindfulness journeys. We enjoy common bonds that I will remember and treasure forever.

Sabbe sattā sukhi hontu! ("May all beings be well!")

Namaste,
LISA

This page intentionally left blank

SECTION 1

Gain/loss,
status/disgrace,
censure/praise,
pleasure/pain:
these conditions among human beings are
inconstant,
impermanent,
subject to change.
Knowing this, the wise person, mindful,
ponders these changing conditions.
—Buddha Sutra

This page intentionally left blank

CHAPTER 1

WHY CMOS ARE FACING EXTINCTION

> *To act without knowing why; to do things as they have always been done, without asking why; to engage in an activity all one's life without really understanding what it is about and how it relates to other things—this is to be one of the crowd.*
>
> —Meng Tzu (Mencious)
> 379–289 BC

Many moons ago, hordes of marketers roamed the Earth. They hunted for fresh ideas, advertising accolades, and brand genius.

Then the Internet-saurus Rex arrived, threatening their very survival. Suddenly, they faced several new predators. Those predators are challenging the role of today's marketing leader as we know it. Left unchecked, some chief marketing officers (CMOs) may possibly face undue stress, and even extinction. I believe it is essential to pay attention to these trends and predators now, and here's why:

1. *Budgets are shifting.* In 2012, Gartner Group predicted that CMOs will spend more on information technology (IT) than chief information officers (CIOs) by 2017.[1]
2. *Lines of responsibility have blurred across functional groups.* CMOs can no longer rely on their creative and business generalist abilities. Nick Eades, who at the time was CMO of the mobile technology firm Psion, stressed that "there's still room for the creative side of marketing, but without a data-centric approach, it would not have a proper context."[2] Will CMOs

choose to hoard their budgets, or create cross-functional teams with IT and sales to build initiatives that drive community-wide mind share and market share?
3. *Social media exacerbates cross-departmental and customer tensions.* Changing social norms, fueled by social media, have caused unprecedented departmental tensions, and are driving CMOs to shift from pushing their ideas to listening more proactively to their ever-expanding community. In the world of transparency, how many companies can truly say that they are in control of their brand, message, pricing, and product quality?

In public, they may proclaim themselves to be brand stewards. In my private CMO peer group discussions, however, leaders tell a different story. I hear countless examples of how their top-producing salespeople monopolize their field marketing teams' time. Their chief executive officer (CEO) meddles in their marketing planning efforts, undermining the CMO's role and authority. It is not uncommon to hear that people outside of the marketing department will offer their opinion on how marketing should be run, which campaigns need resources, and what social media platforms the company needs to pursue. This results in a never-ending pile of last-minute projects, end of quarter "one-off" collateral (such as custom presentations and events), and other potential costly distractions. How does a CMO know which last minute requests are worth completing, and which are windmill-chasing exercises?

4. *The "Wild West Web" spawns confusion and trust issues.* How can CMOs intelligently process and filter through the nonstop cacophony from Facebook, LinkedIn, customer forums, and countless media outlets? For example, in today's over stimulated information marketplace, anyone can become a blogger and a self-proclaimed expert in their field. I saw this trend take shape in 2002, when masses of displaced executives became fitness, life, and business coaches. All they needed to do was promote their services and launch a website to qualify. The same pattern has emerged with the "social media expert" movement. Whom can you trust, and who are the real experts in your field?

Thanks to the era of customer and employee transparency, anyone can proclaim themselves to be a marketing expert, fueling further mistrust and misunderstandings about the true purpose of marketing. Conversely, most employees would never walk into the chief financial officer's (CFO's) office and tell her how to redesign their income statements.

5. *Traditional industries are under attack.* Rapid shifts in buyer behavior and leaner methods of distribution and delivery are spreading across many industries like wildfire, and are forcing marketers to explore new (and uncharted) ways to go to market—and, in some cases, they are barely surviving. Think of the following industry examples:

   - *Book publishing options have mushroomed.* In the days of yore, authors worked through traditional publishing channels: literary agents would vet your book proposal and find you a publisher for a percentage of book sales. Publishers would provide copy editors, production, and public relations teams. In other words, they were the manufacturer and primary warehouse for hard copy books. You, the author, built a marketing plan to promote the book. The sequence was clear and predictable.

   Today, self-published authors can outsource these roles to online firms and freelancers and generate an impressive-looking finished product. Bestselling business authors Seth Godin and Guy Kawasaki chose the self-publishing route in response to disappointing interactions with bulk distribution of their e-books. In Kawasaki's case, retailers such as Amazon and Barnes &Noble could not fulfill an order for 500 electronic copies of *Enchantment* for his upcoming keynote presentation. That inflection point spawned a new bestseller for Kawasaki and coauthor Shawn Welch entitled *APE: Author, Publisher, and Entrepreneur.* Today, many authors love the ability to determine their own publishing fate, and Amazon has emerged as a self-publishing powerhouse for that audience.

   - *Brick-and-mortar retailers are painfully adapting to customers' new buying habits.* JC Penney, Macy's, Target, and Barnes & Noble are watching profits erode because many shoppers visit a brick-and-mortar store to find what they need, then go online for the best price. This nascent customer behavior is referred to as showrooming. In early 2014, JC Penney and Macy's announced thousands of layoffs and dozens of store closings as a desperate yet necessary response.

- *"Almost instant" taxi service is now the new norm.* Thanks to companies like Taxi Magic and Uber, passengers can find the nearest sedan, know their exact wait time, and ride in a comfortable, clean, well-maintained vehicle. The days of waiting outdoors in the rain to hail a cab are disappearing.
- *E-learning and online education methods threaten the hallowed halls of higher education.* Massive Open Online Courses, or MOOCs, have created a new delivery method for learning, and people are enrolling in droves. A January 2014 LinkedIn article discussed a woman named Laurie Pickard who expects to complete her MBA online within three years—for less than $1,000. Columnist John Byrne reported that "in the space of just nine months in 2012, from February to November, the number of institutions offering free online business courses has doubled to 51 from 26, according to the Association to Advance Collegiate Schools of Business (AACSB) International. The number of business faculty teaching MOOC courses has more than doubled in the same timeframe to 83 from 39."[3]
- *In health care, the sick-care models are being replaced by patient-centered care—and, ultimately, prevention-based models.* Hospitals in the United States are particularly poised for radical change. The rapid pace of patient care management technology, the abysmally high medical error rate in today's hospitals (e.g., preventable fatal infections), and our crippling health care costs are literally killing off health-care organizations. They include hospitals, insurers, and private doctor practices. Authors David Houle and Jonathan Fleece describe this dramatic shift in *The New Health Age: The Future of Health Care in America.* They believe that "such change will be so transformational that by 2020 one in three hospitals will close or reorganize into an entirely different type of health care service provider."[4]
- *Stand-alone gaming product sales are declining.* According to management consultant Dan Markovitz, "they are getting crushed by inexpensive, smartphone-based apps. Who

wants to pay for an expensive X-Box that you can only play at home in your living room, when you can spend $1.99 for an app that you can play anywhere, anytime?"[5]

If this level of disruption can happen to CMOs in these seemingly disparate industries, then it can happen in your industry.

Are you taking a broad view of your market potential and competitive landscape? Or do you face market contenders who barely existed a few years ago, and have been operating under the radar? It's possible you have cogs in the value chain that are headed for the endangered species list.

6. *Pressure to demonstrate a return on investment with marketing has reached a fever pitch.* This came to light when I recently spoke with the CMO of a large nonprofit headquartered in Washington, DC. He lamented the cost and the challenges associated with measuring marketing return on investment (ROI). "When I seek approval for my key initiatives from the CEO, she wants facts and figures. I cannot always prove the return on our marketing investments in the short term. A lot of what we do is unchartered territory. And our Google Analytics tools can only tell a partial story. We are stuck between a rock and a hard place because we would love our online efforts to drive more revenue, but we cannot afford the high-end marketing analytics software."

Although the Web has spawned some useful, free tools and apps, many Software as a Service (SaaS) vendors within the marketing analytics field are still able to report double-digit growth and healthy profits. Marketing leaders can choose from a variety of reliable products from Adobe, Oracle/Eloqua, Marketo, and SAS Institute. Their biggest challenge is determining what marketing value and contribution really mean to their organization, not which tool to select. We dive more deeply into the marketing ROI debate in later chapters.

7. *Lines of responsibility across marketing and sales are disintegrating.* According to sales guru Neil Rackham, many companies now expect marketing teams to drive transactional sales growth. Sales no longer own that role exclusively. IBM and GE Solutions are starting to do this. In a recent issue of *Marketing Week*, Rackham explains that "GE Solutions has split its marketing into 'upstream' and 'downstream' groups. The upstream

group focuses on product development, and the downstream group focuses on working with the sales teams." Rackham posits that the downstream group "can create a lot of the tools and wisdom which can help the sales team to add value and select the right opportunities in the consultative process."[6] I'm witnessing the same trend with my CMO peer groups. Nearly half of my members come to the annual budget negotiating table with their sales counterparts and, in lieu of reviewing the value or revenues they can contribute to the overall business, they are assigned a budget that represents a fraction of the total percentage of total projected annual sales. In some cases, that percentage is anemic—as low as 1% or 2% of revenues.

8. *Big data is driving democratized decision-making.* The nascent state of the data scientist profession illustrates how quickly marketing must adapt and restructure teams. New studies are beginning to prove that big data-driven companies can average a 6 percent increase in profits and a 5 percent increase in productivity.[7] In chapter 5, we will explore how big data is affecting marketing behaviors, customer relationships, and investments in greater detail, as well as its limitations.

    As a result of this massive movement, a new culture of decision-making is emerging. In many cases, collaborative decision-making is replacing top-down, intuitive decision-making. This style of decision-making was traditionally relegated to the smartest, most seasoned person at the table. Those days are disappearing quickly. You can thank the "Wild Wild Web" and big data for this ineluctable trend.

9. *Senior marketers worry about staying relevant.* When I surveyed and interviewed 45 senior marketing leaders in late 2012, I asked them about their top challenges. I expected that big data and marketing analytics demands would make it to the top of the list. I was wrong. The biggest marketing leadership obstacles included

    - a lack of self-management structures to help them stay focused and refreshed;
    - persistent cross-departmental conflict, particularly with the CEO and sales; and
    - low technology acumen in areas such as search engine marketing, social media, and marketing analytics.

In spite of the growing need for senior marketing leaders to become more tech savvy, data driven, and strategic, many still feel as if they are playing second string in customer circles and the C-suite. Department leaders habitually reach out to them on an ad-hoc basis, requesting one-off events, short-term campaigns, and last-minute marketing collateral and support to help close a sale. As one CMO peer member told us, "We are tired of our marketing team being treated like a McDonald's drive through window."

Second-string status becomes even more pronounced for marketing leaders who are new to their roles. The infographic in figures 1.1–1.2 summarizes our survey findings.

Figure 1.1   Survey of CMOs

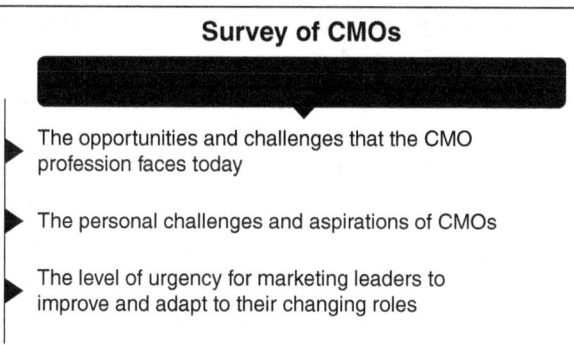

Copyright 2013, Lisa Nirell. All rights reserved.

Figure 1.2   Point 1-Final

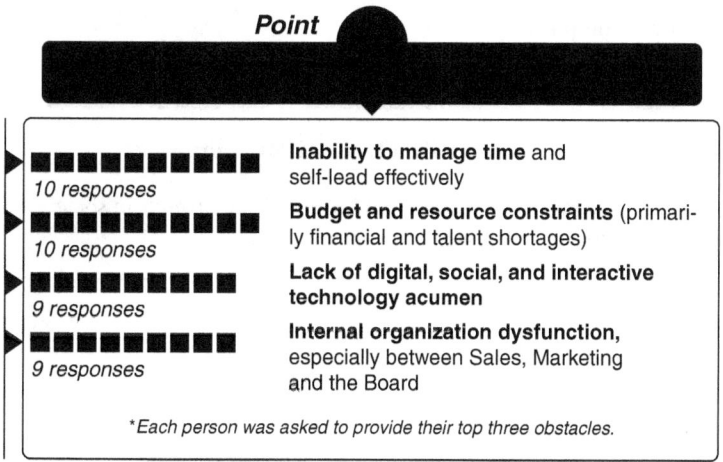

Copyright 2013, Lisa Nirell. All rights reserved.

Where can marketing leaders go to get answers, when many of these technology trends are not being taught in today's universities or executive education programs, and the roads are not yet traveled? How do they allocate time to pause, ponder, and plan when so much change is happening so quickly?

The natural tendency is to work harder, hire more people, and DO more. But frankly, this just fans the "overdoing" flames.

I am concerned about CMOs. Left unchecked, these game-changing trends will threaten the role of marketing in most organizations. I believe marketers need to gain greater influence and impact in today's organizations. I want them to thrive and rise above the online noise.

We need empowered, energized CMOs to tap into their innate talents and teach stakeholders the power of building customer-centric communities. This is only possible if they fortify their own self-confidence, critical thinking abilities, and personal desire to weather the changes ahead. Breakthroughs like this happen when they create a sacred space for new ideas to emerge.

Every one of us who fulfills as marketing leadership role needs to find our *Inner Marketing Guru* (IMG). This book will, in three discrete sections, provide you with tools, ideas, and inspiring stories to guide you on that journey.

This is a unique opportunity in our history for marketing leaders. Who else can balance these newly minted skills as adroitly as today's leaders? They have direct access to customers, the executive team, the external marketplace, and sales channels.

Dinosaurs may have become extinct, but marketers don't have to follow the same path.

INNER MARKETING GURU Inquiry #1:

What are my top five resources for identifying trends in society, our customer base, and within my organization?

CHAPTER 2

THE DARK SIDE OF DATA DEMOCRACY

In this world, there was nothing scarier than trusting someone. But there was also nothing more rewarding.

—Brad Meltzer, The Inner Circle[1]

Every day, my inbox is graced with mass email messages. For your reading pleasure, I have copied a message verbatim:

> From: Marko [mailto:marko@xxx.net]
> Sent: Monday, June 24, 2013 3:43 AM
> To: Lisa Nirell – EnergizeGrowth LLC
> Subject: Re: Post Suggestion for energize growth
>
> Hi Lisa,
> I was just looking for some new material to read on Google on happened to get to your site!
>   Here are some posts we did, let me know if you think we could be suitable for your blog, I would love that.
>   http://abc.com/how-to-improve-conversion-rates
>   http://def.com/10-strategies-for-monetizing-your-blog.htm

Who can take these messages seriously? Few business professionals do. Yet these questionable internet entrepreneurs keep sending this bushwa, so someone must be responding to them!

This email message is one example of how the Web fosters a level of democracy and free speech that we have never witnessed before. We see it in business, and we see it in politics. The Arab Spring was ignited by online postings and messaging, and those oppressed by militant governments are now speaking out. Malala Yousafzai, the fearless Pakistani teenager turned education activist who survived an assassination attempt by the Taliban, addressed the United Nations in 2013, calling for world leaders to protect rights to education.[2] She symbolizes the spirit of free speech and the impact it can have in many corners of the world.

Nobody can silence the ineluctable march of transparency. That's the bright side of democracy.

Then, there is the dark side. Anyone can proclaim themselves an expert in online forums. In fact, you can become a globally recognized blogger within days or weeks. As we have seen with reality TV "celebrities" such as Nicole "Snooki" Polizzi and Alana "Honey Boo Boo" Thompson, online notoriety does not always require intelligence. Nor does it necessarily enrich people's lives. I simply find most reality programming questionable and shady.

Today's democratized Web spawns confusion and trust issues for corporations as well. Today, your competitors can launch a blog or a white paper and quickly reach expert status in their field. I saw this trend take shape in 2002, when masses of displaced executives became coaches. All they needed to do was promote their services and launch a website to earn that moniker. The same pattern has emerged with the "social media expert" movement from 2006 to the present.

You can find plenty of information, but you cannot always trust the source. For many of us staying centered while information buzzes around us can pose a challenge.

Figure 2.1   The Information Buzz

Courtesy of graphic illustrator Toni Glover.

THE DARK SIDE OF DATA DEMOCRACY

As a marketing leader, whom can you trust? Who are the *real* experts? And, more importantly, what is the root cause of this erosion of trust so that we can deal with it in a preventive manner?

When I filter information from my own online channels—email, LinkedIn, private CMO forums, Facebook, and Twitter—I generally feel as if I have no control over what I will find nor what people will say about me. While I would never compare my level of notoriety with corporate chief executive officers (CEOs) or media celebrities, I can imagine they share my sentiments.

The democratized Web is not stopping for anyone. That is the new marketing reality that we must accept, and we must act to minimize its impact.

I spoke with Adrian Ott, a seasoned marketing strategist and author of the bestseller *The 24-Hour Customer*. She works with top technology firms such as Symantec and HP. Here's her perspective on the Web's information smorgasbord:

> *We are in an era of too many choices competing for too little time. The proliferation of products from around the globe has resulted in a plethora of options for buyers. As a result, the concept of traditional customer loyalty has suffered continuous decline from the time when our grandparents "always bought Fords." A study by the CMO Council and Pointer Media Network further reveals that 80 percent of loyal brand sales are attributed to only 2.5 percent of shoppers, not 80/20 as previously thought. Marketers need to find a better way.*[3]

In light of these new Web realities, and the implications for how we relate to our communities, senior marketers need to ask, "*What strategies will help us earn and preserve our customers' and stakeholder's trust, regardless of the communications channel?*"

Before you answer this question, consider the challenge from two angles:

1. establishing and keeping trust with your **customers and prospects**; and
2. establishing and strengthening trust with your **internal team**, such as your chief financial officer (CFO) and CIO

HOW DATA DEMOCRATIZATION AFFECTS CUSTOMERS

Consider how customers think and buy. They are barraged with information, pop-up windows, and content about new products, shopping offers, and special promotions. When confronted by large quantities of information, what will they normally do? They will delete the message (or blame their lack of response on their overflowing SPAM folder). In fact, in chapter 7, we explain scientific evidence that proves most mere mortals can only process between two to four ideas at one time. The sheer volume of information makes it very hard to keep a customer's attention, let alone their loyalty.

While we cannot blame the erosion of customer trust and loyalty completely on the abundance of online information, we can certainly name it as a key contributor. Customers have become increasingly more discerning about what they purchase and the brand behind it. This is causing marketing leaders to work much harder to earn and keep the hearts and minds of potential customers.

What are the best ways to earn and keep customer trust and attention? Today, marketers have many choices. Every marketer will select a different attention-grabbing strategy. This strategy, in turn, shapes every marketing program and helps prioritize investments. Here are a few to consider:

1. *Scavenger hunting.* Using the Global Positioning System (GPS), companies such as Foursquare create a sense of mystery and gaming. Highly active users who check into a favorite hotel, restaurant, or club compete for the coveted "mayor" designation.
2. *Diagnostics and surveys.* In exchange for your providing information about your company, Hubspot will show how your website compares to your competitors for no charge. Symantec's marketing team created a benchmarking tool called INFORM (**INFO**rmation assurance **R**isk **M**odel) to help CIOs assess their information technology (IT) risk. In exchange for answering a survey about their security, compliance, and management practices, respondents could compare themselves to other companies and rapidly identify areas of high risk. Not only did INFORM establish Symantec's thought leadership position but it helped their developers discover new product ideas.
3. *Making your customer a star.* Articulate, an online learning solutions provider, has invented the E-Learning Heroes community where over 107,000 professionals gather to share templates, victories, and learning ideas.

4. *The Greater Good approach.* The "triple bottom line," socially responsible mantra that Seventh Generation, Tom's Shoes, and Clif Bar have integrated into their operations shapes their brand. These companies are committed to a purpose much greater than themselves and want to create a better world.
5. *Customer wealth builder strategy.* In my opinion, wealth is defined as discretionary time. If you can prove to your customer that you can streamline the time to evaluate, install, and use your products and services, you make them wealthier. You help them create white space on their calendar—a rare and precious commodity these days.

I love these strategies because they stretch our thinking on how we can differentiate ourselves from the customers' "delete" key, as well as from our competitors.

Ott tells us that "traditional economics tends to focus on the time to produce the good (i.e. labor)." The customer wealth builder strategy looks at a burgeoning area that marketing leaders are now embracing: the customers' experience with you. Ott continues by saying, "these consumption-related elements help to determine whether the balance of time and value fall into or out of a favorable position for product adoption. For innovators and marketers, it is not about the TIME value of MONEY, it is about the MONEY value of TIME."[4]

HOW DATA DEMOCRATIZATION AFFECTS YOUR INTERNAL STAKEHOLDERS

A multitude of online sources of market, customer, and competitive data can make any executive an overnight expert. This causes an entirely different set of political and communications barriers for marketing leaders as they acquire new competencies in return-on-investment (ROI) tracking, big data, predictive analytics, social media, and marketing operations.

Even though Spencer Stuart recently reported that the average CMO tenure has doubled from 23 to 45 months[5], there is still plenty of evidence of CMO distrust in the executive suite.

Joe Payne, former CEO of Eloqua (now owned by Oracle), validated the source of ongoing tensions and distrust in the C-suite. After spending several years with Verisign, MicroStrategy, and Coca-Cola, Joe became the CEO of Eloqua in 2007. Joe has led organizations in both a CMO and CEO capacity. This makes his perspectives even more noteworthy. Joe has a natural affinity and compassion for the CMO role. In Joe's words, "The CMO role can be the least respected in most companies. This perpetuates the 'CEOs are from Mars; CMOs are from Venus' mentality."

Payne outlined several behaviors that create tension between the CEO, CFO, Vice President (VP) of Sales, and marketing leaders:

1. *Data is the new black.* Payne commented that "what's different today from ten years ago is that businesses used to run on hunches of smart people. Today, you can still play your hunches, but you can test your assumptions. Every aspect of the business today collects more data than ever before. The data to support a direction is always available." As a marketing leader, how often do you seek evidence, benchmarks, and industry data to support your position versus just your gut and experience?

2. *Marketing leaders revel in their use of unique language.* While the CFO and the VP of Sales report on pipeline, revenue, backlog, and ROI, marketing uses different language, such as campaigns, lead scoring, social media, publicity buzz, and events. This causes dissonance with other functional leads in the organization. Dissonance can lead to misunderstandings, and misunderstandings can lead to mistrust.

3. *Marketing is out of sync with the reporting cadence of the rest of the organization.* Most organizations follow a reporting cadence that is weekly, monthly, quarterly, and annually. Think about the staff meetings you attend. The VP of Sales reports how you are tracking against forecast. The CFO reports on how earnings, revenues, and renewals compare to previous quarters.

   Conversely, the VP of Marketing may report on the latest Twitter campaign results at one meeting, and the number of leads from a big trade show at the next. The milestones don't change at random intervals. Marketing should learn to report metrics regularly and consistently.[6]

If any of these behaviors sound familiar, then you are swimming against the current within your organization. In Section 3, I will outline strategies to help you secure your seat in the power circle without needing a life preserver.

> **INNER MARKETING GURU Inquiry #2:**
>
> What is the ideal strategy to gain and keep our peers' and customers' attention and earn their trust?

This page intentionally left blank

CHAPTER 3

GOING DIM: CAN YOU SEE (OR HEAR) ME NOW?

Concentrate the mind on the present moment.
—Buddha

"Craig, will you please turn off your phone while we eat lunch?"

While I briefly felt like a mother scolding her young son, somebody had to say it. Craig, one of my largest clients, personified the overcommitted, stressed-out technology executive. Whenever we met, his phone would ring incessantly, and his eyes would dart in various directions across the room.

Craig's addictive phone habit reflected a deeper, more persistent issue. Craig just could not relax. He spent his 70-hour work weeks behaving like the perfect corporate employee—always engaged with his team, always responsive to the CEO's requests, and always helping close the next enterprise software sale. He was profiting from the technology boom times—it was 1999—and he was one of the most trusted executives at one of the fastest growing, publicly traded technology companies in the United States.

Within months of that lunch meeting, Craig checked into an executive wellness program due to his dangerously high blood pressure and other life-threatening symptoms. He has been on medication ever since he began the program.

How many of us are letting technology infiltrate our lives and dictate our every move, ultimately robbing us of some unique, fleeting life experiences?

I'm going to be blunt. I find it downright disrespectful for my peers to regularly glance at their phones while we steal a few precious minutes of meaningful conversation. Yet, somehow, we feel as if we owe this mobile device our undivided attention. The device isn't a child, a pet, a preprogrammed robot, or a sick friend, yet it earns a place by our bed stand. Sometimes, we even give it a seat at the dinner table.

This is especially perplexing for me, because none of my friends or business peers regularly deals with life-and-death situations. Yet, in most marketing circles, this obtrusive behavior has become the norm. Walk into any meeting or conference, and survey the participants. How many people are clutching onto their mobile devices, only half-listening to the presenter or meeting facilitator? Did they not get the memo that multitasking is actually counterproductive?

I refer to this trend as the *Digital Intrusion Movement* (DIM).

The DIM phenomenon has far-reaching implications, namely in two ways: the **personal effectiveness of marketers erodes**, and **customers get short shrift.** Here are five indicators that leaders are headed to a DIM place:

1. *Health and vitality lose to speed, flexibility, and 24-hour access.* Think about the executives who encourage more technology usage, speed of execution, and "flexible" work hours. (The term "flexible" is often left to interpretation, and is also often perceived as synonymous with "always available to work.") Adrian Ott warns us that customers expect us to always be at their beck and call in her book *The 24-Hour Customer*. Change management guru Daryl Conner reminds us that leaders must be *Managing at the Speed of Change*. Marketing leaders begin to feel that speed is always the answer, that if you are not "Leaning In," as Sheryl Sandberg wants women to do, you're clearly wasting your prime career development years.

Here is another way that these shortcuts have affected our quality of life. The August 2013 issue of *The Economist* took a contrarian position on the "faster and more" theme in their article "In Praise of Laziness":

> "The biggest problem in the business world is not too little but too much—too many distractions and interruptions, too many things done for the sake of form, and altogether

too much busy-ness.... A survey last year by the Centres for Disease Control and Prevention estimated that almost one third of working professionals get six or less hours of sleep each night.... Good Technology, a provider of secure mobile systems for businesses, found that over 80 per cent of survey respondents continue to work after leaving the office, 69% cannot go to bed without checking their email, and 38% routinely check their work emails at the dinner table."[1]

Was *this* the promise of productivity we expected?

2. *Communications shortcuts open the door to misunderstandings and malevolence.* When time is suddenly viewed as precious, and you're somehow wasting it by reflecting or quietly eating your lunch, what happens next? Some people look for communications shortcuts with their peers and customers. We see it expressed through the ludicrous acronyms that have infiltrated our vocabulary and electronic conversations. Just consider these terms, most of which did not exist ten years ago:

- IMHO (In My Humble Opinion)
- LOL (Laugh out Loud)
- TTFN (Ta-ta for now!)
- LMAO (Laugh my Ass Off!)

These shortcuts, when used often, can reduce our ability to really listen to what is NOT being said in a conversation. Our total listening capability erodes.

Suddenly, marketing—which is perceived as the communications command center of today's organizations—is using language that does not fully express the feelings and meaning intended for any given interaction. We are telling the recipient that we simply do not have time for a voice-to-voice discussion, let alone a face-to-face connection.

Malevolence also thrives in the digital social laboratory. For example, Alan Weiss, CEO of Summit Consulting, hosts several online forums for consultants and experts across the globe. He regularly receives emails from acerbic web trolls who criticize him for misspelling a word or for sharing his worldview.

Weiss believes that "the web enables the cowardly. They disguise their comments to critique the people whom they could never become themselves. They say that 'No one knows you're a dog on the internet.' Believe me, dogs act with more integrity."[2]

The worst part is that many web trolls will not come forward in any offline forums and reveal themselves.

3. *"Me too," not breakthrough innovation, prevails.* Count the number of self-proclaimed social media experts and agencies who have appeared on the scene since 2005. Senior executives often tell me sad tales of their five- and six-figure forays into social media and big data initiatives, only to report that they have little to show for their efforts. In lieu of scheduling more face-to-face customer meetings, they are spending time learning how to use LinkedIn's special features or attending the same conferences as their competitors. In many cases, the "experts" and analysts are encouraging them to do so.

This type of activity does not guarantee more customers. But it does guarantee you will have a lot more people randomly endorsing and liking you. This herd mentality further fuels the DIM movement and can waste a significant amount of time.

4. *Reduced face time with customers.* Over the past 14 years, I have been running my own business consultancy and publishing firm. During that time, I have witnessed an increase in the "hide-and-seek" game. I can recall dozens of situations where key executives with C-level positions refuse to answer their phone, schedule face-to-face meetings (unless facing a crisis), and cower behind their keyboard. They will not extend the courtesy of returning a phone message, nor will their assistant. I encountered this challenge with an events planner who helped organize webinars for a multi billion dollar technology company. He asked me to be an expert speaker at an upcoming program, but refused to speak on the phone. He chose to lambaste me using text messaging, and never responded to my voicemail to help resolve a simple misunderstanding.

To gauge your company's natural tendencies, ask your top five executives what percentage of their time is spent every month in front of customers, attending customer events and briefings and calling customers versus responding to emails, LinkedIn requests, and text messages. You will either be pleasantly surprised or shocked.

5. *Customers and stakeholders get shortchanged.* When speed and cost savings overshadow the quality of the customer experience, you repeat the mistakes that Dell reported in 2004. They initially believed that moving technical support and call center jobs to Bangalore, India, would boost share price and save money. They also believed that they could overcome the language and cultural barriers by providing the new Indian team members with two weeks of training. It took Dell a few years' worth of lost market share, nonstop customer complaints, and competitive battle scars to recover.[3]

THE FUTURE IS NOW

Not all online social norms and prospects are DIM. I am encouraged by the leaders who are looking for ways to restore harmony between our digital lives and our humanity. These are a few examples that inspire me, and give me hope for the future.

1. LinkedIn's CEO, Jeff Weiner, believes that generating double-digit growth is a shallow and unsustainable goal. During his speech at the Wisdom 2.0 Summit 2013 in San Francisco, he declared, "Our purpose at LinkedIn is to create economic opportunity for people. If we do it right, then revenue growth will naturally happen. This is very well aligned with managing compassionately." Weiner's organization now serves over 277 million members and has 26 offices.
2. Padmasree Warrior, Cisco chief technology and strategy officer, spent 19 years working on increasing her meditation time from two minutes to twenty minutes daily. She dedicates her unplugged weekends to family, haiku, and painting. She said these activities help her maintain the big picture and a broader understanding of humanity—not to mention her customers.
3. Joseph Hoar, former commander in chief of the United States Central Command (CENTCOM), sat next to me during a flight home to San Diego, California, in 2001. We enjoyed

discussing world politics, his extensive military career, and the good life in Southern California. I asked Joe one question that elicited a response that will stay with me forever. When I asked him the secret to his decades of successful military service, he told me he dedicates time every day to quietly reflect.

4. Tony Schwartz, author of *The Energy Project*, spent two weeks off the technology grid in the summer of 2013. Here is what he learned from that experience:

"The most common reason many of us feel compelled to answer e-mail constantly is that we are addicted to feeling connected. And by the end of two weeks, I couldn't resist checking e-mail any longer, even knowing that if anything critical arose, my office would find me.

"What I know now is that nothing terrible would have happened if I had stayed off longer. Many of us want to believe we're more indispensable than we really are."[4]

Living a DIM lifestyle creates suffering and isolation. When we look our source of suffering straight in the eye, we gain a new understanding of its power over us. That awareness is the first step to transforming today's unsustainable, unhealthy social norms. Section 2 will outline several strategies to help you restore digital harmony.

INNER MARKETING GURU Inquiry #3:

Are our digital marketing initiatives and habits creating chaos or alleviating stress in people's lives?

CHAPTER 4

RETURN ON MARKETING INVESTMENTS: A FLIGHT RISK?

Fortune sides with him who dares.
—Virgil

In chapter 3, we discussed the negative personal impact of succumbing to the Digital Intrusion Movement (DIM). It's unfortunate to let the DIM interfere with your personal effectiveness; it's downright *tragic* to go DIM with your organization's measure of marketing performance and success.

Recall the fatal example of overreliance on technology. On a sunny July 6, 2013, morning, Asiana Airlines Flight 214 entered final approach at San Francisco Airport. With four pilots in the cockpit, the jet was cleared to land with visual approach on runway 28L. At the time, the Instrument Landing System (ILS) (glide slope) on 28L was out of service.

Sadly, things went terribly wrong, terribly fast. Asiana's pilots approached the runway 40 knots slower than the recommended landing speed, resulting in the tail falling off, a cabin fire, and the loss of three lives.

In the days that followed, some experts and authorities speculated that Asiana's pilots have a reputation of being overly reliant on instrument-guided landings, and inferred that the faulty ILS may have caused the calamity.

How many marketing leaders depend heavily on analytics and spreadsheets to track progress with their customer-facing and demand generation initiatives? In my experience, overreliance on these analytical instruments is a recipe for too many *go-arounds*—a pilot's term for aborting a landing and returning to the flight pattern for a second try.

Marketing's probability of budget *pilot error* has been heightened by the increased pressure to grow budgets—often without adding the appropriate resources to support those newly approved initiatives. In 2012, executive search firm Korn/Ferry surveyed 124 of their top executive clients. Forty-eight percent said that Marketing is being given too little budget to do what they need, and forty-two percent said that Marketing was being given enough budget to perform their function. Korn/Ferry's sample set of clients is nearly split down the middle as to how much budget is sufficient and whether Marketing is being set up for success. The study hints that in today's corporations, few people can agree on how much marketing budget is sufficient—and how it should be allocated.[1]

I predict that marketing budgets will continue to be scrutinized and be more fluid than they have been in the past. Marketing leaders need to know what trends will cause them to regularly reevaluate priorities:

- *Explosive growth in marketing automation solutions.* The advent of analytics to make informed strategic decisions, profile customers more accurately, and track campaign results now provides marketing leaders with powerful decision-making ammunition. Companies such as HubSpot, Adobe's former Omniture product suite, Oracle/Eloqua, and Marketo are current industry darlings. The category has spawned a brand new function known as marketing operations. Boards of directors love these products. So do CEOs and CFOs.
- *Increased receptivity to fuel integrated marketing efforts that blend online and offline elements.* While digital budgets are growing, many marketing leaders also continue to invest a healthy portion of their budgets in offline events. These may include exclusive breakfast seminars, user conferences, customer appreciation events, and awards programs.
- *Reduced reliance on information technology (IT) for day-to-day direction and support.* Most of today's marketing operations, lead generation, and data analytics tools are cloud based, so IT

is not needed to install and support them. In fact, they may no longer own the budget for any of these initiatives. Marc Benioff, CEO and founder of Salesforce.com, is known for coining the company mission "The End of Software." This moniker resonates within his company as well as within Salesforce's monolithic partner ecosystem. During their annual Dreamforce user conference, tens of thousands of participants attend. Very few are pure IT professionals.

- *A mindset shift from program management to testing, learning, and creating.* Companies are emerging from a cautious investment spell fueled by the Great Recession of 2008–2010. While this is a refreshing transition, it requires marketing leaders to shift their thinking. Today, they need to view themselves as innovators, not program managers. Many new technologies, such as predictive analytics, are not yet mainstream. They require a *big bet* mindset. Not all leaders are accustomed to embracing this level of risk. But those who are willing to create a marketing innovation slush fund are reaping rewards.

Jim Lenskold, founder of marketing return-on-investment (ROI) and measurement consultancy Lenskold Group, outlines an approach to strategic experimentation to help marketers shift in that direction:

> The key to successful experimentation is managing the balance of testing vs. implementing your "best" plan. You want to ensure that the process of experimentation does not have a noticeable negative impact on results and financial contribution. You are testing high-risk, high-return strategies but the net impact [of testing run in place of standard marketing] should be neutral. First of all, the experimentation is typically delivered to only a small portion of the target audience. Secondly, there is a good probability that the experiments generate just as much positive lift and negative shortfalls to net even. Finally, the experimentation should not have much of an incremental cost with the exception of losing some efficiency...
>
> Each company will need to find its own balance of testing but one split to consider is allowing 20% of your budget for testing slight variations of low-risk and about 5% of the budget for experimentation of high-risk, high-potential strategic

alternatives. That leaves 75% of your budget dedicated to the market plan that consists of the best-known strategies.[2]

Leaders define success differently today than when industrial-age accounting methods were adopted. Older definitions of marketing success, such as number of qualified pipeline leads, conversion rates, market reach, sales pipeline velocity, and event attendance, just don't provide the full picture.

The demise of corporate giants WorldCom, Enron, and Adelphia taught us that strong market share, political power, and money do not necessarily translate into sustainable market leaders. Conversely, these events were also a blessing in disguise, because they prompted boards and executive teams to demand clearer accountability standards from every department in their organizations. Finance, Sales, and Customer Service are expected to deliver against a set of metrics and standards. What makes Marketing immune?

I believe the traditional marketing metrics I mentioned above, such as qualified lead volume and pipeline velocity, lack depth. They prevent us from designing a holistic way of thinking about long-term marketing performance. In other words, they undermine our ability to strike a more meaningful balance between marketing success, revenue growth, employee happiness, and customer evangelism—the essential ingredients to a strong brand. This broader view has prompted innovative companies to redefine market success. This is why the Customer Experience movement, the American Express Global Customer Service Barometer, and Frederick Reichheld's Net Promoter Score have earned a seat around the marketing performance table.[3]

Once marketing leaders acknowledge these opportunities to grow their budgets, support an increasing number of strategic programs, and measure marketing on a much broader scale, what happens next? Most leaders will naturally forge ahead, confidently navigating across departmental lines and engaging customers in their new initiatives. Yet expanded authority does not give marketing leaders license to fly at unsafe speeds or altitudes. Strategic, mindful leaders need to anticipate what obstacles they may encounter in their flight path. Here are the most common obstacles I have seen:

1. *Under-estimating potential turf battles.* In one instance, one CMO confidentially told me that "keeping our customer data base

current is very important, but it is currently owned by several departments. Not one person is accountable; it's a committee effort. Nobody feels they have enough resources to manage it."

In another example, the CEO of a fast-growth technology company told me that she has repeatedly witnessed the growing tensions between CMOs and IT. Their firm provides products and services to help Fortune 500 companies accelerate market share by generating relevant, real-time customer and competitor insights.

The CEO shared that "we are seeing more scenarios where Marketing owns the budget, and many IT departments are feeling left out, and less influential.

"In one of our largest accounts, a multibillion dollar industrial company, we are seeing tremendous tension. Our primary buyer, the VP of Marketing within a large business unit, is in the process of introducing Customer Relationship Management [CRM] and big data analytics. The IT department was never consulted during the evaluation and selection processes. Now, they are behaving badly.

"My account team participated on a call with both IT and Marketing, and the IT department said, 'You are not allowed to install the tool because it has not yet been vetted.' In other words, Marketing had not performed the proper IT procurement steps."

Imagine how many weeks of productive, meaningful customer face time were forever lost due to this turf battle within their customer account!

2. *Lack of clear attribution.* Some companies lack clear metrics attribution, especially between Sales and Marketing. Double-dipping can occur when sales and marketing report the results from a given campaign. Dominique Hanssens, professor of Marketing at the University of California, Los Angeles (UCLA) Anderson Graduate School of Management, posits that "attribution can sometimes cause double accounting, particularly with TV ads and follow up sales."[4]

3. *Short-term mindsets on the true value of Marketing persist.* In the United States, Accounting standards do not allow Marketing to be put on the balance sheet as an asset. So Marketing is treated as an expense, even though some Marketing initiatives

impact long-term brand repute, customers' propensity to buy more products from you, and a company's cultural clout. *Forbes* columnist and MarketShare director Daniel Kehrer observed that "marketing expenditures are technically an expense, as opposed to an investment, and that's an issue here. In finance-speak, marketing costs are a P&L [profit and loss] item, *not* a balance sheet item."[5]

Hanssens also reveals that most companies focus too much on *flow metrics*, which can include weekly sales and comparisons of revenues over time and lead conversion rates. He recommends companies also consider *stock metrics* in their performance management systems. These can include future income streams such as brand repute and value, the value of inventory, and the quality of the customers you are attracting.[6]

What about your company? Are you selling to buyers who are going to be loyal, long-term customers, or to buyers who, like Groupon and LivingSocial have demonstrated, chase daily deals? These online discount sites exemplify the longer term impact of an obsession with flow metrics and quick transactions.

In chapter 27, we discuss and present some new definitions and models that will not only expand your view on the value you create for your organization. You will also learn how other marketing leaders are creating greater impact on their company's revenue and brand repute. The upcoming frameworks will ensure you don't run your best-laid marketing plans aground.

INNER MARKETING GURU Inquiry #4:

How can we shift our internal conversations from "what drives revenue" to "what creates lifelong customers and brand repute?"

CHAPTER 5

BIG DATA OR BIG DISAPPOINTMENT?

Computers are good at swift, accurate computation and at storing great masses of information.... The brain's strong point is its flexibility. It is unsurpassed at making shrewd guesses and at grasping the total meaning of information presented to it.

—Jeremy Campbell[1]

My first corporate job out of college opened my eyes to the power of personal computing. As a 21-year-old, I never dreamed how much data would become a cornerstone of today's modern marketers.

In 1984, I was appointed the International Marketing and Sales Director for one of the world's first PC software companies, MultiMate International. Rick, my boss, gave me a Compaq Portable computer to take home and use. He secretly hoped I would spend my free weekend and evening hours crunching spreadsheets, writing sales letters, and learning DOS (operating system) commands.

I recall lugging that boxy, 20-pound computer up the stairs of my parents' home and staring into the tiny screen. Wow! 256K of RAM and two floppy disks to store my content... how could I possibly use all of that space? I felt like a member of the technology elite. It was a powerful machine—or so I thought at the time.

Today, we are dealing on a whole new realm of data. Big data "farms" transmit more information across the Internet every second than the total amount of data stored in the entire Internet in 1992.[2]

The term "big data" burst on the scene just a few years ago, and has reshaped how we view customer relationships, reporting, lead scoring, fraud detection, and other commercial applications. Data scientist talent is highly valued, and the role is still being defined by organizations and academic institutions.

How did big data become such a hot trend, and how will it impact today's marketers?

First, let's define it. *Big data* is the process of analyzing and implementing actionable intelligence that helps companies achieve new levels of efficiencies, profits, and customer relationships. Big data-driven decision-making is different from traditional data analytics in three ways:

1. *Volume:* Big data applications collect and analyze petabytes of data. This is enough data to fill millions of filing cabinets worth of text.
2. *Velocity:* The speed of processing real-time information is often a competitive advantage in highly commoditized businesses, such as credit card companies and airlines. Today, some major credit issuers are using big data to reduce fraud detection times from 45 minutes to as little as four seconds.
3. *Variety:* The power to synthesize information from a multitude of sources. You can incorporate data from voice, online surveys, social networks, mobile devices, and the Global Positioning System (GPS). Today, people who carry smartphones and tablets might as well consider themselves walking data centers!

Carousel30, a digital marketing agency based in Alexandria, Virginia, recently summarized the explosive growth of big data.[3] Big data initiatives can ostensibly improve the customer experience and accelerate marketing programs such as

1. *Product development.* Today's marketers can gather disparate data: voice, survey summaries, social media commentary, free-form commentary (also known as "unstructured data), and online and online customer forum content to identify key themes. These themes help them determine unmet customer needs.

2. *Predictive customer modeling.* Imagine a mobile provider who can deliver right-time offers based on location and past purchase history. Retailers such as Amazon have pioneered personalized online shopping experiences based on a customer's profile.
3. *Resource planning.* Indian online travel agency redBus uses big data to plan resources and maximize efficiency for things like which routes need more buses, patterns in customer demand fluctuation, the management of resources for booking requests and so forth.[4]
4. *Personalizing customer interactions.* Vision Critical, a cloud-based software and services company based in Vancouver, Canada, for example, uses big data technologies to enable two-way communications with communities, customers, and employees. They gather and manage surveys and peer-to-peer discussions for over 600 customers, and manage over 2.5 million customer survey initiations per month. Their work with NASCAR, highlighted in the box on the following page, showcases big data's impact on their fan base.
5. *Custom content creation.* Most e-commerce powerhouses such as Netflix and Amazon use big data to power recommendation engines and personalize our shopping experiences. In August 2013, LinkedIn joined the personalized content ranks when they launched University Pages. This service helps institutions create custom content, searches, and other functions that provide a unique and data-driven resource for the user. The user and technology communities applauded them for the time they invested in studying user needs and designing an application that provided high value.[5]
6. *Natural language processing.* Big data processing power can help companies gather huge volumes of voice, video, and written customer feedback to help them analyze and take action on the results. This helps organizations assess and respond to changing market needs at never-before-seen speeds.

   For example, in the data-intensive healthcare industry, natural language processing can be can be used to analyze a physician's patient notes. Then it can help predict the likelihood of hospital re-admittance.[6]

HOW VISION CRITICAL HELPED NASCAR IGNITE A BIGGER FAN FOOTPRINT

Situation: Five years ago, NASCAR's chairman mandated that Marketing launch a brand initiative to attract the next-generation audience in order to increase viewership and sponsorship. At that time, after decades of steady growth, NASCAR's attendance and TV ratings began to drop. NASCAR hired Steve Phelps as the CMO, and he swiftly revamped the entire marketing department. He immediately decided to leverage the existing NASCAR Fan Council to help drive decisions such as changing game rules and launching the Gen 6 car.

Reigniting the Fan Council: *Official NASCAR Fan Council* is an insight community where avid fans provide feedback on how to improve the NASCAR experience. On average, NASCAR engages members at least twice a month on specific topics that influence everything from the on-track competition to business to marketing decisions. In 2008, NASCAR partnered with Vision Critical to create this community of 12,000 passionate NASCAR fans. Giving fans a voice requires no additional incentive; the fans feel honored and take pride in being a part of this advisory board, which has led to extremely high response rates for most studies.

Results: Research tripled while research costs decreased by 80 percent. Fans regained their voice, leading to key changes to the sport itself. And, in 2011, TV ratings and viewership increased for the first time in three years.

Not only have these benefits paid off for the company and its relationship with fans but they have also earned NASCAR and Vision Critical the prestigious Forrester Groundswell Award for listening to consumers and generating business results using social media. Tyler Douglas, Vision Critical CMO, added, "with the Fan Council, we were able to create ongoing dialogue with thousands of fans that culminated in a substantial amount of data. Through Vision Critical's analysis, not only were we able to mine the big data collection for quantitative feedback, but we were able to pull *qualitative* insights that allowed us to make sound recommendations to elevate the NASCAR fan experience."[7]

Improved fan engagement using social media and big data drove higher NASCAR financial performance. And they are not alone. In the October 2012 issue of the *Harvard Business Review*, Andrew McAfee and Erik Brynjolfsson delineated the distinctions between data-driven companies and intuition-driven companies, and the positive business results that data-driven firms can typically generate. In 2012, they interviewed 330 public North American companies to learn how they applied data-driven decision-making to improve corporate performance. Here is what they learned:

> *The more companies characterized themselves as data-driven, the better they performed on objective measures of financial and operational results... companies in the top third of their industry in the use of data-driven decision making were, on average, 5% more productive and 6% more profitable than their competitors.... It was statistically significant and economically important and was reflected in measurable increases in stock market valuations.*[8]

With results like these, how could anyone possibly argue *against* the merits of big data?

The Gartner Group has. They are a large, established analyst firm with technology industry gravitas. Jackie Fenn, a Gartner fellow, has been publishing an annual *Hype Cycle for Emerging Technologies* report. In the 2013 edition, she declared that big data has reached a stage that she called The Peak of Inflated Expectations. In other words, she considers big data as hype. Gartner predicts that another five to ten will pass before big data reaches a "plateau of productivity." This represents the time required until a technology can be readily and easily adopted.

On the other side of the debate you will find International Data Corporation (IDC). Their 2012 report predicted that revenues in the Apache/Hadoop-MapReduce software market will grow more than tenfold by 2016. Hadoop is an open source software project that allows huge data sets to be processed across many clusters of commodity servers. Sometimes, data spreads across thousands of servers. The benefit is reduced reliance on high-end servers.

When two research behemoths could not come to terms on big data's merits, I became skeptical. After I spoke with numerous leaders of failed or delayed big data projects, I was convinced of big data's limitations.

For example, through my research and interviews I learned that many companies consider big data as a top priority, yet the number of successful projects is not yet significant. Infochimps, an Austin, Texas-based technology consulting firm, joined forces with SSWUG.ORG, an information technology (IT) professional member organization, to learn more about the market trends. They surveyed 300 senior technologists in fall 2012.[9]

The survey respondents, mostly IT staff members and managers, represented companies ranging in size from fewer than 100 to over 1,000 employees. While they reveal that 81 percent of the respondents consider big data initiatives one of their top five priorities, 55 percent of big data initiatives are never completed, and many others are falling short of their objectives.

Here is one more reason to be wary of its promises. Big data server farms could be missing more than half of the information about your customers. Alexis Madrigal, a contributor to *The Atlantic*, revealed in October 2012 that, in *The Atlantic*'s case, 56.5 percent of social traffic sources remained invisible to data analytics programs. She named this the "dark social" phenomenon:

(Dark social) shows up variously in programs as "direct" or "typed/bookmarked" traffic, which implies to many site owners that you actually have a bookmark, or typed in www.theatlantic.com *into your browser. But that's not what's actually happening a lot of the time. Most of the time, someone Gchatted someone the link, or it came in on a big email distribution list, or your dad sent it to you.... Dark social is even more important across this broader set of (media) sites. Almost 69% of social referrals were dark.*[10]

I am not suggesting that companies should abandon big data initiatives designed to accelerate growth initiatives. Nor am I recommending that organizations complete every big data initiative they launch, just to prove something. Perhaps, during the early stages of these projects, companies find the project is fruitless. I can conclude from these surveys, however, that a sizable number of companies are now taking big data initiatives seriously. But "seriously" does not equate to "successfully."

By the way, are you tired of reading all of these facts and figures yet? I thought so. Before you jump to the next chapter feeling exasperated, I invite you to consider that big data is not a game changer. It's a tool with a finite set of benefits in a marketing leader's toolbox. You don't have to go far to find its limitations. Just look inside our own heads.

Neuromorphic engineers have been working for decades to design a computer that works in ways that go way beyond marketing analytics. They ultimately want computers to act like and operate like the human brain. Our brains have three characteristics that computers cannot yet emulate:

1. Brains consume little power (20 watts versus supercomputer megawatts).
2. Brains have a high fault tolerance. (computer microprocessors crash when one transistor breaks; our brains lose neurons regularly without significant consequences).
3. Brains don't need programming; they adapt to changing demands, stimuli, and environments. Computers operate from fixed algorithms.

In my opinion, here's where the big gap with big data lies: **The ability to clone human consciousness is elusive to us mere mortals.** Our brains are organized in the visible lobes and ganglia of the brain. That's where our 86 billion nerve cells (neurons) reside, and where human consciousness performs its magic. Yet, with all the scientific grants and "big brains" dedicated to neuromorphic engineering, nobody has yet figured out how neurons are organized within these areas.

HUMAN CONSCIOUSNESS, LOOSELY DEFINED

Look in your favorite dictionary. Surf the Web. You will be hard-pressed to find a universal definition of consciousness. Consider this one, and keep it if it works for you.

Consciousness is an umbrella term to define the human experience. This experience can appear in many layers. The first layer describes *ordinary consciousness*, such as an awareness of your body (which we share with most living creatures); *self-consciousness*, which is being an observer of your own life experiences; and *universal or cosmic consciousness*, which author Richard Maurice Bucke defined as "an awareness of the life and order of the universe, possessed only by enlightened humans" in his magnum opus, *Cosmic Consciousness: A Study in the Evolution of the Human Mind*.[11]

As we fast forward to today's highly automated and interconnected society, we explore consciousness through several lenses. These include the study of consciousness through the lenses of spirituality, philosophy, psychology, body-mind connection, and neuroscience. Big data does not scratch the surface of these realms.

Big data-driven marketing initiatives come with other inherent limitations as well. Consider these before you embark on a costly program:

1. *Expect major resistance if your organization prides itself on a culture of intuitive decision-making.*
2. *Big data cannot provide business context to analyze the data and take meaningful action on it.* We still need intuition and discernment to interpret and prioritize.
3. *Avoid biting off too much with a big data initiative.* "Scope creep" will surely alienate other departments and delay quick wins, leaving the project vulnerable to cancellation and suspicion.
4. *Be careful to ask the right question(s).* This can quickly derail the project, and could send you in the wrong direction with customers. Additionally, humans naturally suffer from "observation bias." This is the opposite of having an open mind that is unfettered by rigid thinking. If something does not fit into our rigid way of thinking, we normally blame it on an outside force as opposed to the way we think.
5. *Listen carefully to your intuition.* Have you ever walked into a meeting and felt that something was awry—yet you could not put your finger on it? Did you pause, observe, and adjust, or did you ignore it? Jill Richards, former CMO of Terracotta Technologies, reminds us that "The answer is not always in the data; it's based on what you know about how people and markets work. In the end, people buy from people. There is still a 'trust your gut' factor. Sometimes the market timing may be off. Maybe the market or internal team is just not ready to hear it."[12]

Arianna Huffington, founder of *The Huffington Post*, takes the intuition argument one step further. She believes that "Our world has become unmanageable. We go from crisis to crisis. Many of our challenges, such as sequestration and the fiscal cliff, are manufactured. Many people with very high IQs are making very bad decisions. What's missing is wisdom."[13]

In every business decision you make, you should consider its impact on your customers, community, and culture. Are your data-dependent investments contributing to chaos or alleviating stress in people's lives?

As of this writing, big data (thankfully) cannot emulate our higher levels of consciousness and inner wisdom. These include the ability to express sensations, emotions, and feelings in response to experiences, and to feel that we are inextricably linked to something greater than our physical bodies. And experiences, often seemingly random, are what continue to enrich our lives, our human relationships, and our customer interactions. Over time, those experiences fuel our wisdom.

As I recall the mornings when I opened that Compaq personal computer box, walked down the aisle on my wedding day, and made my first six-figure software sale, I realize how these events significantly contributed to my own body of world wisdom. No Hadoop server farm will ever reproduce those moments.

> **INNER MARKETING GURU Inquiry #5:**
>
> How will we strike a balance between big data and wisdom in our highest priority marketing initiatives?

This page intentionally left blank

CHAPTER 6

MARKETING AND SALES: A HARD LANDING

> *Equanimity is one of the most sublime emotions of Buddhist practice. It is the ground for wisdom and freedom... (it) arises from the power of observation, the ability to see without being caught by what we see... (equanimity) can also refer to the ease that comes from seeing a bigger picture.*
>
> —Gil Fronsdal[1]

If John Gray had continued publishing bestsellers, I have the perfect title for his next book: *Marketing Is from Mars; Sales Is from Venus.*

Metaphorically speaking, I have lived on both planets. A few decades of experience helped me realize that the oxygen levels, landscape, and temperature were vastly different on each one. During my early career days in the 1980s, I performed both roles for an Ericsson spinoff company that competed against IBM and Compaq for desktop market share. It was a race to capture market share and a high-stakes career opportunity. The term "equanimity" never entered my mind in those early days.

Later, I joined BMC Software and spent equal time in both functional areas. My four years with OnTarget, later purchased by Siebel Systems (now Oracle), required that I open a new market from scratch—with limited resources. Marketing acumen played a critical role during my first two years on the job and helped me grow my practice from $0 to $1.2 million.

By 2002, I launched my own consulting firm and flew away from the Siebel corporate nest. I have been working with hundreds of entrepreneurial marketers since then. If there has been one constant throughout the past 30 years, it has been the persistent tension I've witnessed between Sales and Marketing teams. That tension is especially acute within business-to-business (B2B) organizations.

I once heard an executive say, "When the water is low, the rocks appear." Today, the rifts between Sales and Marketing rise to the water's surface as an increasing number of my CMO clients are assigned sales quotas. Up to that point, many of them had never held a sales position, which means that most of them have limited knowledge of the process of selling. This leads to missteps and unnecessary tension with other sales channels. Assigning a CMO a sales quota without providing the necessary sales education and increased customer face time is a recipe for greater tensions.

I finally began to see organizations acknowledge and address these challenges when companies shifted their focus from hoarding cash to reinvesting in growth. Thanks to the early successes with marketing automation (also known as the marketing cloud), companies have seen some improvement in the quality of their sales leads, the prioritization of leads, and an improved ability for Sales and Marketing to share a common language around their customers' buying behaviors. Nonetheless, some old beliefs and behaviors, which I will explain further in the coming pages, still prevent marketing leaders from earning the respect of their revenue-producing and financial counterparts.

Over the past decade, I found three factors that, when ignored or downplayed, create the most friction between Sales and Marketing: **Data, Roles,** and **Content**.

Figure 6.1   Sales and Marketing Harmony Formula

Copyright 2013, Lisa Nirell. All rights reserved.

DATA DROWNING

The first disrupter to Sales and Marketing harmony is *data interpretation*. In many cases, Marketing and Sales are operating based on multiple views of the truth. Brian Kardon, CMO of software provider Lattice Engines, notes that "when the CEO wants to accelerate the company's rate of growth, she might call a meeting with the head of sales, CMO and CFO. However, the VP of Sales, CMO and CFO are typically referring to three different systems to assess where they are. The VP of Sales brings in data from the CRM [Customer Relationship Management system]. The CMO uses data from the marketing automation system (if they have one). And the CFO presents data from the company's financial system. Very often, these three systems give very different pictures of where the company is. This makes it virtually impossible to determine what the challenges and opportunities are."[2]

To make things more complicated, these three executives often disagree on the data itself—the size of the pipeline, average sales cycle, pipeline velocity, and brand repute (which is difficult to measure, yet essential for long-term success). As a result, each executive delivers a single view of the big picture.

Defining appropriate data owners and their *roles* can also be tricky. In B2B marketing circles, several CMOs have established models to track and improve how they create demand. Think of this model as a sales funnel on steroids. The model usually shows the different ways a lead can be generated: by a salesperson, through inbound marketing or an effective piece of marketing content, or as a "bluebird." It also includes terminology that tells you whether that lead was generated by Marketing, Sales, a channel partner who qualified the lead, and so forth.

Unfortunately, the process model does not make it easy to juggle the sheer number of handoffs between Marketing, Sales, and Customer Service that naturally occur during the life cycle of any customer. In some instances, companies allow Sales and Marketing to jointly claim ownership of the customer relationship. (I equate this to companies who firmly believe in hiring co-CEOs. I think this is rarely a success). While the demand creation process model is a noble attempt at aligning teams around the customer, it doesn't make it easy for the *customer* to know whom to call when problems surface—let alone for a company to determine who really owns the customer relationship.

Data definition can also run amok. In many companies, Marketing defines sales leads one way, and Sales defines them another way. Charles Gold, a seasoned CMO based in Washington, DC, observes that "When sales and marketing define target markets, leads and opportunities differently, then everyone loses. I've seen the scenario where marketing proudly reported that they generated 1,000 leads, and sales argued that they weren't actually *leads*, but rather *names*. Then both parties pull out different reports with different numbers to argue their case."[3]

In addition, companies do not always distinguish between *buyer experience* and *customer experience* during planning and status meetings. This can be especially troublesome when you have prospects who are not yet ready to buy, or will never buy from you. If a buyer chooses your competitor, yet they still engaged with you for certain stages of their buying experiences, then they still had a buying experience that is worth noting! In some cases, the buyer might not make it to a final purchase.

One of my colleagues has been an exit-planning expert for small business owners since 1994. He regularly meets CEOs who express interest in selling their business, and ask for his help to optimize the valuation and find ideal buyers. Many sellers get cold feet, and years may go dark until they get serious about the transaction. He operates his business in a small metropolitan area. People don't tend to move away from that region. If he were to walk away from those prospective buyers, or stop sending them valuable marketing content, they might choose to never buy from him, let alone engage in any buying experience when they are really ready to sell.

How does marketing ensure that the future buyer continues to have a positive experience with your company, even when Sales and Marketing have ostensibly fulfilled their roles in the buying process? Down the road, they will remember that experience. When multiple departments are involved, consistency and speed are at risk.

Data availability, or a lack thereof, also contributes to misalignment. When a company creates a new market category, Sales and Marketing often lack historical insights into the way buyers behave when they buy. In some circles, this is also known as the *buyer profile* or *buyer persona*. In these scenarios, Marketing's role is more chaotic and less formulaic than for companies selling into an established buyer community. It could be easy for Sales to become frustrated with Marketing's "test and learn" approach—yet they often have no choice.

Mike Troiano, CMO of data storage company Actifio, illustrates this dilemma:

Actifio is a disruptive technology, and our primary marketing challenge is that we solve a problem most customers don't yet know they have. Our marketing needs to work on two levels, and the first is an umbrella effort to educate the market about the "copy data storage" problem.

Building awareness of that problem simply takes time. In the interim, we need to make sure we're generating the leads we need to drive revenue growth *right now*. To do that we've defined an efficient model of generating a flow of near-term opportunities by leveraging our channel partner relationships, and our Inside Sales team is a crucial part of that formula.[4]

ROLES

Sales and Marketing roles can be viewed from three angles: their respective *missions, accountabilities,* and *collaboration.*

When I worked in a corporate Marketing setting, it was not uncommon for Marketing and Sales to focus on different goals and operate with different **missions**. My marketing programs team focused on new product revenues over a one-year horizon, and program efficacy (number of new product trials) was a leading indicator of future success. Sales, on the other hand, was incentivized to hit quarterly revenue targets, and was not rewarded for selling our entire product suite.

Avangate's CMO and Senior VP, Marketing and Products, Michael Ni, has found **accountabilities** to be a problem. "Sales teams are deal-oriented with fast closes while marketing tends to be more investment-oriented, creating very different perceptions of their senses of urgency. Marketing's current premise is built around longer payback horizons that may not always seem immediately tied to sales' needs, and vice-versa."[5]

Sales and Marketing **collaboration** also has room for improvement, even in today's interconnected world. How many Marketing teams can claim to have earned Sales' trust when it comes to developing messaging and selling playbooks? Apparently not as many as we had hoped today's technology platforms would deliver.

In November 2013, cloud-based business presentation company Brainshark revealed highlights from their *State of the Sales Rep* survey. They surveyed salespeople from a variety of industries and sizes. For any marketer, the results were sobering. The survey revealed that one in three sales reps (33%) are "often" or "always (on a daily basis)" frustrated by their inability to quickly locate sales materials. More than one in five (22%) say they would "need a GPS to find the materials [they] need."[6] Even in today's wired world, organizing the right materials for the right prospect at the right time can be chaotic and time consuming.

CONTENT

The third element required for harmony is **content.** This is defined as information that educates, inspires, and engages your prospects and customers. The four key considerations are *quality, sources, delivery,* and *shelf life.*

Content *quality* should be your first priority. It's our job as marketing leaders to escape from providing ho-hum content that looks like our competitors'. Where can you find inspiration to accomplish that?

Let's turn to cable television for some answers. For the past five television seasons in the United States, actor Bryan Cranston played Walter White, a hapless chemistry teacher turned megalomaniacal crystal methamphetamine maker in the TV series *Breaking Bad.* The writers single-handedly created a brand new genre they call *cowboy drama.* This series exemplified compelling, groundbreaking content, which *Breaking Bad's* creator/executive producer/writer/director, Vince Gilligan, invented. The network, AMC, created many different online forums where viewers could interact with the writing team throughout the five seasons, establishing a perpetual content-marketing machine. Millions of fans voted "yes" with their remote controls.

If you're not feeling like you are a television series genius of Gilligan's ilk, you can create powerful content by synthesizing and simplifying ideas for your customer base. They need help sifting through reams of data and will reward you handsomely as an aggregator.

Also, rethink your *content sources.* Don't accept the belief that Marketing needs to only generate their own internal team of subject matter experts. Over time, marketing cannot drive awareness, interest, demand, and retention without leaning on their ecosystem. That's an inefficient use of marketing resources. Instead, I recommend that marketers employ a plethora of sources, including product marketing, analysts, external experts and authors, customers, customer support, and sales. They can become part of your Content Management Pool,[7] as highlighted in Figure 6.2.

Figure 6.2   Content Engine

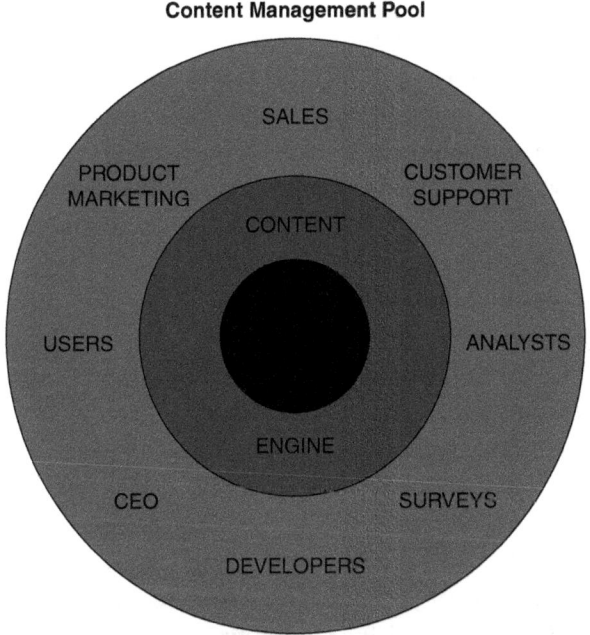

Copyright 2013, Charles Gold, used with permission.

Content delivery can also differentiate you from the crowd and help Sales gain more traction. Consider the multitude of new ways you can deliver the same content. It's easy to get comfortable repeatedly using the same content-marketing strategies. Thanks to agile marketing methods and "test and learn" models, marketers can experiment, measure, and retool rather quickly.

MarketingProf's 2013 Content Marketing Trends[8] study revealed that today's B2B firms typically manage 12 marketing tactics at one time. The top-five most effective tactics used today are social media outlets (not including blogs), articles, eNewsletters, blogs, and case studies. Companies who want to stand apart from the crowd and make sales teams productive should seriously consider short webcasts, executive breakfasts, e-books, screencasts (using tools such as Articulate's Studio[9]), and educational videos.

The belief that content has a *shelf life* is a myth. Today, some of the best content can influence prospects for months, if not years. One of my clients, ON24, publishes an annual Webinar Benchmark Index,[10] the first of its kind. Their findings derive from their database of more than

20,000 customer webcasts delivered within a 12-month period. Industry experts and customers often rely on the annual updates to design, launch, and measure the results from their own events.

If these three areas are left unchecked, they will trigger ongoing conflict where it hits the hardest: in the marketers' and salespersons' wallets. Historically, the sales leaders to whom I reported often thought they could solve most Sales and Marketing problems by tweaking compensation plans. In my opinion, this is akin to waxing your car because your engine is rattling.

That does not downplay the need to review compensation programs regularly. As a leader, you have to trust that compensation will be perceived as fair, as long as you continue to launch great products, pursue new markets, and foster a healthy, customer-centric culture.

Sales and marketing teams may never reach perfect alignment. In fact, some tension can be healthy. It can not only encourage the company to thrive in their learning zone, but it also forces companies to continually assess whether their sales and marketing practices are designed in the best interests of their market. Assessment and observation will help marketing leaders reach equanimity.

In chapter 10, we will review additional ways to achieve greater equanimity between Sales and Marketing teams. At a minimum, Marketing can equip sales organizations with conversation starter tools. These help build rapport in the early phase of the customer buying cycle. Bestselling author Jill Konrath, the author of *SNAP Selling* and *Selling to Big Companies*, developed these sample questions for the VP of Sales, her targeted prospect:

1. *Knowing that it's been a tough year for many in your industry, how big of a stretch will it be for your sales organization to meet your numbers?*
2. *Since most of my clients are struggling with new client acquisition and long sales cycles. I'm wondering how big an issue this is with your sales team?*
3. *What are you doing to re-tool your sales force to increase their effectiveness with today's savvy prospects who have minimal tolerance for anyone who wastes their time?*
4. *How long are you going to skimp on investing in sales force development—especially when it's well known today that they're your primary differentiator... not your product or service?*

5. *What are you doing to help your sales team create fresh opportunities out of thin air?*[11]

Build a method for fine-tuning your relationship with data, content, and team roles. Worry less about who gets credit, and more about how the customer can benefit from your industry leadership. These adjustments will hone your concentration skills, which is a step in the right direction toward finding your *Inner Marketing Guru*. This way of thinking will prevent you and your customers from slipping on the river rocks.

> **INNER MARKETING GURU Inquiry #6:**
>
> What are the biggest causes of dysfunction between our Marketing and Sales teams, and which ones must we eliminate immediately?

This page intentionally left blank

CHAPTER 7

MULTITASKING MASH-UPS AND MISHAPS

> *Managers who believe that frenetic activity is the hallmark of innovation may be making a serious mistake.*
> —Teresa Amabile, Harvard Business School professor and coauthor of The Progress Principle[1]

It was just a dent on the bumper. But it left an indelible mark on my approach to work.

While driving through a torrential rainstorm last year, I called a client to tell her that I would be late for our meeting. Calling her while stopping at a traffic light made perfect sense at the time.

When the light turned green, I immediately put my foot on the gas. There was only one problem. The cars in front of me hadn't yet begun to move. I slammed into the SUV in front of me, triggering a very angry look from a tall driver. He walked up to me, surveyed the minor damage, gave me a stern look, and returned to his SUV.

His steely glare was a wake-up call. That was the day I stopped texting and checking emails while driving.

Texting while driving is one of many examples of multitasking. It's an insidious and often illegal habit. While we may believe that taking part in a variety of tasks at one time provides efficiency and greater flexibility, it can lead to tragic outcomes. If you have fallen into the multitasking trap, I'm about to persuade you to escape it. I am hopeful that the following research will change your attitude about multitasking.

When combined, *information overload* and *multitasking* can render even the most intelligent, spry marketing leaders ineffective. *These two habits are the fastest way to block your Inner Marketing Guru.*

These complementary vices are also a reason why so many marketing executives now work two full-time jobs. Here's how their schedule looks. During the day, they attend agency meetings, review progress with team members, study the latest digital trends, and submit status updates to senior leadership. If they are lucky, they may have some time remaining to visit customers.

By nightfall, they begin their desperate attempt to empty their inbox, check LinkedIn for messages, visit their favorite online forums, and perhaps post a photo or comment on Instagram or Facebook. Before signing off for the day, one of my clients sits in bed next to his wife checking emails, discussing marketing trends, and talking about the highlights of their respective workdays.

You call that foreplay?

I have found marketers to commit these common multitasking maladies during all hours of the day:

1. texting during meetings
2. texting while driving
3. Web surfing or typing while talking on the phone
4. maintaining an inordinate number of open screens on their device
5. making every corner of their home an extension of their office activity
6. using mobile devices while participating in social or family activities

I have examples too numerous to mention here, such as the mother who regularly surfs the Web in front of the community recreation center locker room shower area while her children are showering. Another common occurrence is when executives keep using and glancing at their smartphones during an entire lunch meeting.

Why should you seriously consider reducing multitasking? In a nutshell, it significantly hampers your productivity, creativity, and quality of life. First, let's look at four reasons for reducing multitasking from a logical perspective:

1. *Multitasking causes significant economic losses.*[2] Basex, a business research firm, has conducted a study on the impact of multitasking on the U.S. workforce and reported that multitasking is a $650B problem. That number can be attention grabbing, even if you question their hypothesis and cut that productivity number in half to $350B.
2. *Multitasking slows you down by playing tricks on your brain.* Professor Rene Marois and his research team from Vanderbilt University determined that our brains are designed to work on one task at a time. When you switch from one task to the next, your brain goes through a three-step process: it chooses to switch tasks, turns off the cognitive pattern for the old task, and then turns on the new pattern (or rules) for the new one. Marois discovered that areas of the frontal lobe actually cause information-processing bottlenecks.[3] Even though many authors like to draw analogies between parallel processors and computers and the human brain, we *are* different.
3. *Perpetual distraction makes you dumber.* Two professionals who have dedicated their careers to the study of multitasking support this argument. First, Dennis Clayson, a marketing professor at the University of Iowa, proved that students who text during marketing lectures received lower grades. The same marketing students who texted truly believed that they got the "gist" of the lessons, but clearly they did not fully optimize their learning.[4]

Stanford University sociology professor Clifford Nass, who passed away in 2013, was cited by KPBS for his passion around studying multitasking and our relationships to technology. Here's an excerpt from that obituary:

> To anyone who claims they're able to multitask, to concentrate on multiple things at once while still thinking creatively and using their memory, Nass had a ready response. "They're basically terrible at all sorts of cognitive tasks, including multitasking," he told *Science Friday*'s Ira Flatow.

"People who multitask all the time can't filter out irrelevancy. They can't manage a working memory. They're chronically distracted," Nass said. "They initiate much larger parts of their brain that are irrelevant to the task at hand. And even—they're even terrible at multitasking. When we ask them to multitask, they're actually worse at it. So they're pretty much mental wrecks."[5]

4. *It sacrifices satisfaction for speed.* Professor Gloria Mark of the University of California, Irvine, led a study of the impact of email interruptions—one cause of multitasking—in a simulated office setting. Here's what they found:

    Our results show that when people are constantly interrupted, they develop a mode of working faster (and writing less) to compensate for the time they know they will lose by being interrupted. Yet working faster with interruptions has its cost: people in the interrupted conditions experienced a higher workload, more stress, higher frustration, more time pressure, and effort. So interrupted work may be done faster, but at a price.[6]

5. *It forces you to spend more time on each task.*

    I was personally skeptical about these findings, and began looking for exceptions. I imagined that one form of interruption could be a positive influence, and might cancel out the deleterious effects of multitasking. Professor Mark refers to this as "same context interruption." In other words, if two people are working on the same activity, and one interrupts the other with a new idea, this could perhaps foster collaboration.

    I was wrong. Mark found that "*any* interruption introduces a change in work pattern and is not related to context per se. Interruptions that share a context with the main task may be *perceived* as being beneficial, but the actual disruption cost is the same as with a different context. Our results suggest that interruptions lead people to change not only work rhythms but also strategies and mental states.... After only 20 minutes of interrupted performance people reported significantly higher stress, frustration, workload, effort, and pressure."[7]

If the scientific research doesn't convince you to reduce multitasking, the impact on your quality of life and creative contributions just may. Since interruptions cause you to spend more time on each task—many of which involve problem solving and tactical firefighting—you will naturally face more time pressure to complete every task. Multitasking makes you focus on fixing today's problems, not focus on creating tomorrow's innovations. That's the nature of most interruptions. Under these conditions, other aspects of your life, such as personal health, family, nutrition, and creativity will take a back seat.

When you incessantly multitask, you are robbing yourself, your team, and your customers of your innovative and creative best self. This is unfortunate, because marketers have been historically rewarded for their creativity and resourcefulness.

I turned to another behavioral expert, Harvard's Dr. Teresa Amabile, for insights. She has dedicated over 30 years of her career to studying creativity and organization effectiveness. She conducted a study of 177 professionals across 22 project teams. She concluded that "time pressure, although it may spur people on to do *more* work, may undermine precisely the kind of thinking needed to do *creative* work." She also discovered that

1) the greater the time pressure, the lower the intrinsic motivation to complete the work. Passion and self-motivation naturally erode. Research participants felt too controlled by their environment as time pressure increased.
2) the more people felt controlled by their environment, the more they reverted to old patterns of thinking (which she called "familiar algorithms").[8]

Although we can never eliminate multitasking entirely in our daily lives, what would happen if we reduced it by half? What creative, growth possibilities could emerge?

I found some practical ideas to help you immediately reduce multitasking in your marketing organization. First, treat each task like a single prayer bead, as in figure 7.1. Brian Scudamore, CEO of 1800-GOTJUNK, proposes three strategies: "Train your brain to concisely focus on one thing—then switch to the next. Make time with your family and friends to be just that—if you're at the pumpkin patch, be at the pumpkin patch." And, during times that require intense focus, "turn off your phones and email."[9]

Figure 7.1 Treat Each Task Like a Single Prayer Bead

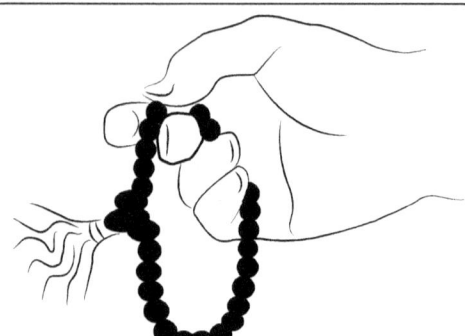

Courtesy of graphic illustrator Toni Glover.

While they are not comprehensive, here are additional adjustments that can add up to significantly less multitasking:

1. *Schedule shorter meetings (20–45 minutes).* To drive even higher productivity and focus, remove the chairs from the room. A Ragan Communications study showed that your biggest time waster is talking with coworkers, so look for ways to streamline those meeting conversations.[10]
2. *Put people ahead of technology.* When someone needs face time, close or turn off your devices and maintain comfortable eye contact. Stand up from your chair and engage in the conversation unfettered by technology. Even better, take a walk together sans mobile devices.
3. *Create focus rituals.* For example, when you need zero interruptions, close your door. Since I have enjoyed life as a virtual entrepreneur for 17 years, I have experimented with other methods. This one stuck: I have a door tag with a bird illustration that says "Nesting." That is a signal to my husband to avoid interrupting me unless it's really urgent.(unfortunately, our cats still cannot read).
4. *Minimize use of any hands-free phone devices in your car.* Realization, a project management technology firm, reports in its white paper that "Mobile phone usage studies show that drivers are seriously impaired while using cell phones... later studies demonstrated that even hands-free devices can cause driving impairment equal to or worse than a .08 percent

blood-alcohol level—the legal threshold for impairment in most states in the U.S."[11]

5. *Find joy in planning.* Realization CEO Sanjeev Gupta reports that "Well begun is half done. If teams have everything (i.e., good design specifications, clear goals and the necessary inputs) in place before starting a project, they encounter fewer questions and issues in execution. The dependence on managers and experts is reduced and work gets done faster."[12]

6. *Drop out.* Find one activity that makes you happy and refreshed, and do it without using any technology. For me, I disconnect at least 30 minutes per day by spending time in nature, relaxing with our cats, meditating, or swimming. Create the time as if your life depended on it—because it actually does. How will your life look different if you just implement one of these strategies? It could be the difference between driving a luxury sedan on the German autobahn and riding in a makeshift rickshaw on a cobblestone street.

INNER MARKETING GURU Inquiry #7:

Where is our marketing team practicing multitasking, and what can we do to stop it?

This page intentionally left blank

SECTION 2

WALK SLOWLY

It only takes a reminder to breathe, a moment to be still, and just like that, something in me settles, softens, makes space for imperfection. The harsh voice of judgment drops to a whisper and I remember again that life isn't a relay race; that we will all cross the finish line; that waking up to life is what we were born for. As many times as I forget, catch myself charging forward without even knowing where I'm going, that many times I can make the choice to stop, to breathe, and be, and walk slowly into the mystery.
—Danna Faulds[1]

This page intentionally left blank

CHAPTER 8

FIND YOUR *INNER MARKETING GURU* TO MAKE BETTER DECISIONS

What lies behind us and what lies before us are tiny matters compared to what lies within us.
—Ralph Waldo Emerson

I do not believe that big data, customer-driven buying cycles and a growing set of job demands cause marketing leadership angst. The real culprit is the impermanence of the marketing profession. And that impermanence, when ignored or underestimated, leads to erratic decision-making, isolation, and unnecessary stress. This can drain even the most accomplished marketers.

While many technology experts and consultants encourage marketers to *do* more, I suggest you need to *be* more. This can be accomplished by pausing, observing, and creating time to regain your balance.

This approach may feel counterintuitive to many marketers. In these competitive times, shouldn't you focus on filling your calendar, just to fulfill your ever-expanding job requirements? That is certainly what I originally believed. In fact, my parents taught me that hard work was the key to success. Now, 30 years and several gray hairs later, I have realized that behavior just fans the "overdoing" flames and, in the long term, accelerates career burnout.

Jon Kabat-Zinn established the Mindfulness Based Stress Reduction (MBSR) Clinic in 1979 to address these Western societal maladies.

Decades later, with a little help from the marketing machines at the Omega Institute and Oprah Winfrey's media empire, both New Age and Main Street acolytes embrace his education programs.

Kabat-Zinn posits that "too much of the education system orients students toward becoming better thinkers, but there is almost no focus on our capacity to pay attention and cultivate awareness. Mindfulness is a way to rebalance ourselves. Instead of being lost in thought, or caught up in emotional upheaval, we can tip the scale in the direction of greater equanimity, clarity, wisdom, and self-compassion by actually learning how to inhabit that other dimension of our being."[2]

The MBSR seminars have expanded to health clinics, mainstream hospitals, and personal growth retreats around the globe. And, true to the mindfulness mantra of "living in the present moment," Kabat-Zinn professes that the programs continue to organically evolve without use of data analytics, rigid planning models, or spreadsheets:

> There was no indication it *(meditation)* would work or that people would be willing to engage in something that, frankly, looked a lot like nothing. Paying attention to obvious things like your breath, or the sensations in your body, probably seemed like a waste of time. Today, people recognize that they're not going to find well-being from the outside, or from a pill; they're going to find it by looking inside.[3]

In theory, this idea makes perfect sense. In practice, it often feels like a pipe dream. Customer deadlines encroach upon our personal lives. Employees and bosses abruptly leave. Corporate boards demand reports and strategy shifts. Customer relationship management systems crash. Parents age and suddenly need our attention. The list never ends.

That's why, in today's crazy-busy world, we need a little extra help. We need to find our *Inner Marketing Guru (IMG)*.

Think of the IMG as our inner guide. Our IMG, as illustrated in figure 8.1, reminds us to pay attention—to be mindful—and to live our lives from one moment to the next.

When working with my CMO clients, breakthroughs happen when they find that IMG. I design my private peer group meetings as a sacred space where new ideas emerge. The group intelligence, or higher power, gives members permission to tap into their IMG. Members unplug from

Figure 8.1 Your Inner Marketing Guru

Courtesy of graphic illustrator Toni Glover.

the urgent. Instead, they focus on designing the future, as well as their own renewal and professional enlightenment.

In my quest to help my clients, I began to apply lessons from my personal self-discovery journey. During that journey, I serendipitously stumbled across the seven Buddhist precepts for awakening.[4] In my experience, they illustrate the IMG concept beautifully.

It will help us to briefly explore each of the precepts, and consider how just *one* of these could be integrated in your daily life and leadership practices. In future chapters, we will delve more deeply into how each precept can be applied to your marketing mission.

1. *Mindfulness* is the art of paying attention to several elements, such as our body, emotions, and mind. An absence of mindfulness severely restricts our ability to learn from our surroundings and from others.
2. *Investigation* is the ability to understand and accept the *dharma*, or the *true nature* of all things. In modern terms, it's your *reality check*. It helps you see things as they really are. When you assume you already know what customers want, or truly believe you can change another person's behavior, you are probably grappling with accepting the nature of things and inflicting unnecessary suffering on yourself and others.
3. *Energy* defines the fuel you need to persistently act. For marketers, this translates into maintaining the will and

persistence to carry out your initiatives and goals, even when you feel discouraged. When I work with clients, I pay special attention to my members' energy levels, their propensity to take action, and how they nourish themselves intellectually, physically, spiritually, and nutritionally.

4. *Happiness* occurs at two levels: In relation to an *object* (which can appear in the form of accomplishments, such as getting a raise, winning a new customer, or fostering productive team relationships), and in relation to *state of mind* (often attained through some form of mindful or spiritual practice). Buddhists believe that we need to cultivate both facets of life. Sustained, long-term happiness emerges when we see things as they really are. Author Piyadassi Thera cautions that "The man lacking in this quality cannot proceed along the path to enlightenment."[5]

How does your organization cultivate happiness? Do you celebrate customer and team milestones, or do you promote long work hours, political intrigue, and nonstop fire drills?

5. *Tranquility* occurs when we are able to attain calming of the body and calming of the mind. Every work environment should include a quiet, technology-free workspace to help us achieve this. Google and the *Huffington Post* offer employees meditation rooms. Employees can use these spaces to nap, meditate, and unplug from the hectic work pace. Numerous studies have revealed that people who work in open, wall-free office spaces are, over time, less productive than those who have a quiet work room.

6. *Concentration* occurs when we can achieve a steady mind and stay strong during times of turbulence and incertitude. Five behaviors obstruct our ability to concentrate. They include sensual desires, wishing ill-will on others, limiting beliefs (also called "obduracy of mind"), worry, and doubt. Something as subtle as how we respond to media interviews provides a lens into these hindrances. For example, some companies invest their messaging in disparaging their competitors versus focusing on how their products and services offer distinctive or breakthrough value. In which camp do you stake your claim?

7. *Equanimity* reflects the capacity to adapt, to let things move and shift. This allows us to change from being rigid to being open to new possibilities. When we are calm and concentrated, equanimity can naturally appear. For example, do you have preconceived notions of how your customers behave and what they need? According to Allie Gray Freedland, PR Director of New York-based iAcquire, "Think of the transference to marketing. We are often clouded by preconceived notions of how we should be communicating with our...customer, even though those notions may not even be relevant or effective. It's just the time-tested way within your organization to do something, so we continue to do it."[6]

These preconceived notions simply cloud opportunity. Freedland continues by saying "many companies have a hard time trekking out of their offices into the 'field' to chat with folks who have firsthand experience with your business—your customers. Having a clean slate or a liberated notion of your customers allows you to uncover brand promises that could be one step away coming right from the mouth of your valued customer."[7]

The art of awakening and mindfulness have provided a competitive edge in several well-established companies. In August 12, The *Financial Times* profiled leading organizations, such as General Mills, Google, Green Mountain Coffee, and Target. Author David Gelles illustrated how they are using consciousness-raising practices—like meditation, mindfulness, and yoga—to develop focused leaders who make better decisions. In fact, 25 percent of large companies now offer some type of stress-reduction initiatives.

Medical evidence also supports the benefits of meditation and mindfulness. As of this writing, you can find over ten thousand studies on the benefits of meditation and mindfulness practices. They are proven methods that reduce levels of cortisol, a hormone that fluctuates based on our stress levels. Gelles shows that "when cortisol levels drop, the mind grows calmer and gains the stability to become more focused."[8]

For thousands of years, practitioners across many continents have expressed the value of mindfulness, but could not show the connection to science. Times have changed, and I'm very excited about living in this era. We can now explore and apply concepts and tools that were heretofore rejected as edgy, "woo-woo," and unproven. Mindfulness is an idea whose time has come.

How can you activate your *IMG* and dramatically improve your decision-making? Here are three ideas to get started.

1. *Watch your language.* Establish a *check-in* process during team meetings to help everyone become centered and focused on the task at hand. For example, when I practice the *check-in* process with my clients, I ask, "What's different?" What worked in your performance? What didn't work in your performance? For what are you grateful?" When you use this specific language, you raise the conversation to new levels. You leave little room for drama, blame, and victimhood. We discuss this process in greater detail in chapter 12.
2. *Let go of the past.* This strategy runs contrary to Jim Collins' *hedgehog model,* which encourages companies to only focus on what they are passionate about, what they do very well, and what the market will reward them to deliver. While many companies reinvest in their hedgehog, they often don't know when to walk away from the past, divest their cash cows, and reinvent themselves. Track how often you begin comments with "*I have worked in this industry/business/company for 25 years, and I know this is true...*" That's a sure sign you are resisting equanimity. I encourage my clients to allocate at least 10 to 15 percent of their budget in unproven, exploratory initiatives. Some create an "innovation reserves" category.
3. *Invest in a trusted peer group.* Find a face-to-face community of like-minded leaders who are committed to supporting one another. By participating fully, you will reap five key benefits. You can test ideas, solve problems, get fresh insights from outside your industry, share resources, and celebrate wins. Chapter 15 shows you some ways to find the ideal peer group and become a productive contributor.

Have you gone through your career running the same tape and script from one year to the next, never realizing you can choose another path? Our *IMG* empowers us to change how we respond to monumental marketing shifts. Conscious communication, present moment focus, and celebrating wins with trusted peers will help you fully experience that freedom. Maybe the Buddha was an enlightened CMO in disguise.

> **INNER MARKETING GURU Inquiry #8:**
>
> What is one thing I must stop doing to create space for my Inner Marketing Guru to emerge?

This page intentionally left blank

CHAPTER 9

WESTERN MINDFULNESS: A BRIEF JOURNEY

Whatever the present moment contains, accept it as if you had chosen it. Always work with it, not against it.
—Eckhart Tolle[1]

Being a marketing leader in today's economy reminds me of my first solo cross-country flight in 1988: even when I think I'm totally in control, bad things can happen.

I prepared one week in advance for this 280-mile adventure from Stratford, Connecticut, to Concord, New Hampshire. I had all of my sectional charts clearly marked, and the weather forecast was clear blue skies and calm air. As I crossed the invisible aerial state border from Connecticut to New Hampshire, something strange happened.

My plane was tracking toward an airport—but it wasn't the Concord airport. In fact, the airport within sight looked very unfamiliar compared to the one on the map: it had two runways. It took me several seconds to realize it was Manchester airport, a military base. Visions of armed military guards greeting me and my Cessna 152 were scary. Even though I had meticulously prepared for this day, I temporarily lost my sense of direction. My plans were almost thwarted, and I nearly panicked.

As our roles as marketing leaders continue to change at breakneck speed, do you ever feel like you are no longer the captain of your own journey? These are trying times for marketers, and our traditional flight plans need revisions.

Mindfulness has emerged as a growing trend in the Western world. Over the past 40 years, we have witnessed a broader acceptance of living in the present moment, which is the essence and definition of mindfulness. Various mindfulness practices, which we will be exploring in this chapter, provide us with a refuge when we want to sustain or regain our balance and sense of direction.

Maintaining a nonjudgmental awareness of our waking moments is possible—even amidst the cacophony of technology, personal commitments, and endless distractions. *How* we attain greater mindfulness in our daily lives as marketers is not the important point here. The continual, committed pursuit of mindfulness is. With practice, it helps reduce stress, improve the quality of our work, and think more clearly.

Let's define the term mindfulness in greater detail, because it is often misunderstood. *Mindfulness is a state of living in the present moment without judgment, which ultimately optimizes our human experience.* At its core are three components: the body (our awareness of our physical being); attention (the ability to observe internal/physical and emotional and external stimuli; emotion (the awareness of our feelings); and our mind-set (the ability to change perspectives toward ourselves through our beliefs and language. When we ignore or suppress any of these aspects, we miss important cues and impose unnecessary suffering on ourselves and others.

In the past 40 years, we have witnessed a surge in studies that prove the benefits of meditation on the brain. It would take several volumes to outline the thousands of studies and the emergence of the contemplative science movement, which is what this nascent area of study is called. Today, organizations such as the Mind & Life Institute and Stanford University School of Medicine's Center for Compassion are discovering the connections between mindfulness practices (such as meditation) and brain function, bringing a whole new dimension of scientific study and validity to the practice.

In the West, many of us may think that mindfulness requires us to commit to hours of seated meditation every week. That's only one approach. We can experience mindfulness through a multitude of channels. The gateway to mindfulness is through body-centered awareness. While this is by no means an exhaustive list, here are several body-centered practices currently used by Westerners:

- *Silent meditation* is available in many forms. Various practices include seated meditation, walking meditation, and

Transcendental Meditation (known as TM). While Jon Kabat-Zinn has excelled at introducing Mindfulness-Based Stress Reduction to institutions of all sizes and types, other options are also available. For example, over six million people have learned TM over the past 60 years, and its efficacy has been supported by over 360 peer-reviewed studies.

Celebrities suchas the Beatles and comedienne Ellen DeGeneres have helped TM become mainstream. Maharishi Mahesh Yogi, the original great teacher of this technique, summarized the benefits this way: "Orderly thinking leading to orderly action improves the behavior of the person and improves your environment."[2]

The only skills required to meditate are a desire to be a better person, to create a better quality of life, and to allocate time to practice.

- *Chanting* appeals to people who find solace and peace in singing. Unlike my experiences singing in a traditional chorus, chanting allows me to lose my self-consciousness about the quality of my voice, how I sound, and how others perceive me. I do my best to match my tone to the group and allow the sound to go where it goes. It is similar to all other physical forms of mindfulness because it requires you to maintain proper posture. This allows the maximum amount of air to enter your lungs, and helps energy, or chi, flow through your body.

  The person leading the chant may select certain words or phrases: the sutra (an excerpt from a Buddhist sermon); a mantra (a repetitive set of words or syllables); a dharani (a longer mantra); or a gatha (a short verse chanted repeatedly). One of the most common mantras is *om mani padme hum*, which has its roots in Tibetan Buddhism.

- *Breathwork sessions* are frequently hosted in a group setting and are designed to relieve stress, reduce physical pain, and relieve past traumas. The programs come in many flavors. I studied breathwork techniques with teachers who have been certified by Dr. Judith Kravitz. Over the past 30 years, Deepak Chopra and Christiane Northrup, two highly respected integrative medicine doctors, have endorsed her approaches. The www.transformationalbreathing.com website outlines an array of benefits from breathwork, such as reducing stress,

promoting higher levels of energy, and releasing negative emotions and trauma.
- *Qigong* has its roots in Taoist Chinese philosophy, and literally translates into "intrinsic life energy." Some acolytes refer to it as qigong, chi kung, or chi gung. Over the past four thousand years, Chinese philosophies and societies ranging from Confucianism to Buddhism to Taoism have adapted qigong to their own styles. Practitioners define it as aligning breath, movement, and awareness for cultivating our intrinsic life energy (referred to as "chi").

  Qigoing combines the wisdom of Chinese medicine, martial arts, and philosophy. Unlike TM, it is difficult to find peer-reviewed studies on its physical and emotional benefits. Individuals practice for a variety of reasons, such activating self-healing and improving their martial arts skills.
- *Yoga*, derived from the Sanskrit word *yuj*, means "to unite or integrate." Yoga integrates the body with the mind and breath through breathing, yoga postures (known as asanas), and meditation.

  Since I began practicing yoga in 1996, I have discovered three forms. Each one offers different health and spiritual benefits. *Hatha*, which is slow and therapeutic, is considered the foundation of all yoga styles and ideal for beginners. *Vinyasa flow yoga* incorporates a series of 12 poses, and shows practitioners how to align each movement to their breath. It helps build lean muscle mass, strength, and flexibility. Some also say it reduces the risk of heart disease, high blood pressure, and type 2 diabetes.

  Ashtanga yoga has also been called power yoga. Teachers often mention the eight limbs, which is a metaphor living a meaningful and purposeful life. The eight-limb philosophy, made popular by Sri K. Pattabhi Jois, is more physically demanding than hatha and Vinyasa yoga. It produces intense internal heat, which is intended to detoxify muscles and organs. Pattabhi Jois passed away peacefully in 2009 at age 93.

  Most Westerners have barely scratched the surface on the benefits of yoga. Sports clubs and rogue yoga instructors concentrate on the physical benefits of the practice, and often stray from the traditional sequence of postures and approaches that gurus have been teaching for over five thousand years. Yoga was introduced to American audiences in the late 1800s, and is still evolving and being adapted to our culture. Nonetheless, it offers numerous benefits. Imagine finding a venue where you can unplug from technology and conversation for an entire hour! This is a precious perk in itself.

- *Tai Chi* (also known as *tai chi chuan*) is considered as a graceful, slow form of stretching and movement that is accompanied by deep breathing. Much like flow yoga, practitioners move from one posture into the next without pause, ensuring that the body stays in constant motion. Some tai chi programs focus on maintaining good health, while others are designed as martial arts enhancement programs. Much like yoga, tai chi is also designed for different skill and physical levels.

When we maintain awareness of our physical bodies, we activate our emotional and environmental awareness. In mindfulness, this encompasses three areas:

1. the ability to observe and identify internal and external stimuli
2. awareness and identification of our feelings or emotions
3. awareness of our mind-set and the ability to change our perspectives

Our awareness is refined and shaped by seven types of filters. Here is a summary of six common filters. Many may sound hauntingly familiar:

1) VALUES

Our values dictate "how we do things" in every corner of our lives. Values around our health and wellness, financial fitness, community, achievements, customer relationships, and quality are just a few categories where our values are expressed.

Beginning in 1990, Harvard Business School professors John Kotter and John Heskett surveyed over two hundred companies across more than 22 industries, and continued the surveys for 11 years. They found that firms with a strong corporate culture based on a foundation of shared values outperformed the other firms by a huge margin in the following areas:

- Revenue grew more than four times faster.
- The rate of job creation was seven times higher.
- Stock price grew 12 times faster.
- Profit performance was 750 percent higher.

This research emphasizes one of the many reasons why I guide entrepreneurial teams toward reaching consensus on values."[3]

2) BELIEFS

Beliefs help us determine our own interpretation of the truth. They can be expansive beliefs or limiting ones. For example, we may believe that all predictive analytics tools are too difficult and costly to deploy based on a previous negative experience. That singular experience does not make it true, however.

In my three decades of selling and marketing, I have discovered several beliefs that limit our potential:

1. "Planning is difficult, time consuming, or expensive."
2. "It didn't work last time (or, it won't work anyway)…so why bother?"
3. "Marketing does not work for this kind of service. Our market/customer base/approach is unique."
4. "I cannot launch this plan until I know exactly what to do." (This belief wins the PMA—the Perfectionist Mindset Award.)
5. "I don't have the right certifications or education to move forward."

3) ATTITUDES

Attitudes reflect your perspective at a given point in time. They can be positive or negative, and are shaped by the other filters I have listed.

4) MEMORIES

Memories are past experiences that shape your current reality. We often use our memories as a way to rationalize our beliefs. Memories are what we *think* happened, and are seldom highly detailed or accurate. Just ask crime witnesses to describe the perpetrator; you will receive a plethora of inconsistent answers.

5) DECISIONS

Decisions usually happen either because a) we faced time pressures to take action or b) were heavily influenced by an outside force or expert to take action. The term "decision" is very different from the term "choice." The decision filter removes a large amount of personal responsibility from the action we have taken. Later, we can say, "that industry analyst recommended this strategy" or "my boss told me to pick something." When we make *choices*, we commit to an action and take full responsibility for that choice.

6) LANGUAGE

Vocabulary is a palpable filter. My mentor and world-renowned consultant, Alan Weiss, says that "language controls discussions, discussions control relationships, and relationships control business." [4] This is true for anyone who wants to persuade anyone to do anything.

Taking this filtering concept one step further, let's say that you have written a brilliant marketing, social media, our publicity plan, but you carry around a set of filters that undermine them and you choose to ignore them. What will happen next? In my experience, applying the same filters to new ideas can limit your marketing and personal potential. Just ask Ron Johnson, the former CEO of JC Penney. He spent 17 months on a brand revitalization effort.

Johnson brought his "design thinking" filters and merchandising approaches to JC Penney from his years of successfully launching cool retail stores for Apple and Target. When he joined JC Penney, he purchased a full-page ad in *The Wall Street Journal*, declaring that they were "dreaming up new ways to make you love shopping again."[5] Johnson's new strategy alienated the majority of traditionally discount-driven customers, who took their spending power to Macy's, Kohl's, and The Dollar Store.

The final piece in the mindfulness equation is emotions. These six filters, coupled with external stimuli, ultimately inform our emotions. A key lesson I have taken from Buddhism is that attachment, or denial of the transient nature of our surroundings, objects, relationships, and emotions, is the cause of much of human suffering.

Buddhism reminds me to detach from my emotions. It is not easy to do, but in most instances, I can identify a negative emotion, then allow it to arise and pass. During several moments of grief and loss, this has been a lifesaver. Imagine how more productive we can be when we can shift, for example, our negative reactions to lost market opportunities or competitive losses, and transform those thoughts into a new, more empowering direction.

MINDFULNESS AT WORK—AND WHY IT WORKS

Christopher Penn, Vice President of Marketing Technology for SHIFT Communications, has incorporated mindfulness into his marketing agency's culture. He reminds us that "there are so many avenues for distraction, from economic reports to constant social media updates, that being mindful and focused is an ever increasing challenge."

Penn's journey to greater awareness has evolved over the past decade. "My own path began several years ago. One of the most powerful practices I learned was a visualization exercise to use before speaking in public. Prior to 2006, when I first attended retreats led by Stephen K. Hayes, I was on stage to market my company, and my talks, while informative, had the wrong motivation—and thus, the wrong energy. After those retreats, I learned a process in which I visualized every word I said floating out into the audience, touching lives, and helping to make things better. Once I changed my motivation from pitching to helping, I worried much less about what people thought of me. It was no longer about me, but the message." His audiences and clients noticed a change, and he was invited back more often to lead marketing sessions and keynotes.

As his practice deepened, Penn began introducing mindfulness meditation to over 110 SHIFT Communications team members in the Boston office. "I've deployed a series of practices, from 10 minute mini-meditation sessions at our offices to even publishing a 6 minute, public domain MP3 for people to use."

SHIFT Communications has seen several positive, lasting outcomes. Penn reveals that "the biggest, most obvious metric is subjective opinion. Do people benefit from the practices? From the teams we've done these practices with, the answer is an unequivocal yes. For the people servicing clients, I've definitely seen an impact in productivity. They are getting more done with less stress—and leaving the office on time![6]

Obsessive goal-setting, lead tracking, and marketing planning need to be tempered with stillness. My countless years telling my clients about the value of tracking measurable results and developing written goals were not spent in vain; however, my approach was missing this essential ingredient. Movement, breathwork, and silence are powerful pathways to fine-tuning our senses, reframing our mind-sets, and sustaining forward momentum.

Instead of waiting a year to schedule a retreat, start now. Schedule ten minutes every day for silent reflection or movement. Before you break into a cold sweat at the thought of a temporary digital detox, remember that this change will not happen overnight. Humans typically need to practice something new for at least 21 days before we form an opinion about its efficacy—that's the magic number of days that scientists say it takes to form new habits.

In the next chapter, we outline the personal attributes that mindful marketers have in common, and more strategies to help you emulate their success. That's a journey worth taking.

INNER MARKETING GURU Inquiry #9:

What mindfulness practices am I willing to integrate into my daily life?

This page intentionally left blank

CHAPTER 10

FIVE TIMELESS QUALITIES OF MINDFUL MARKETERS

Knowing others is intelligence, knowing yourself is true wisdom.
—Lao Tzu

It's one thing to understand mindfulness from an intellectual standpoint. But how do we integrate mindfulness into our daily lives as marketing leaders?

I define a mindful marketing leader as someone who influences the hearts and minds of others to improve their condition, or the world at large. And because information is moving at record speed and crossing organizational hierarchies, it is imperative that marketers influence others in an honest way. After advising executives for over 15 years, I have discovered five timeless qualities of a marketing leader.

1. *Acceptance of who you are.* As agents of innovation and transformation, we are constantly inspiring others to embrace change. It's important to set our intentions so that our best marketing innovations and programs improve our customers' condition and society as a whole. When we deeply understand our natural way of operating in the world, we waste minimal time pursuing some impossible image that we think others want us to portray. We shed ourselves of the exhaustive quest to look good or to avoid looking bad. Our work becomes easier and joyful because we are accepting who we really are.

Before we can reach that level of acceptance, we need to understand and explore the intrinsic aspects of ourselves. Daryl Conner, a 40-year veteran of organizational change, believes it's not just about *what we know* or *what we do*; rather, it's *who we are* that matters most. I couldn't agree more.

Conner explains that when we approach any situation, three aspects of our "persona" are working in tandem:

1. *Technical abilities*: This is what we know, and what we do—Conner refers to this as "the concepts, frameworks, processes, and techniques used when engaged with our constituents." I'm surprised how many professional associations, institutions, and certification programs only focus on nurturing technical abilities. Management consulting firms, for example, often think their methodology is what separates them from competitors. Their websites will often illustrate some cryptic process visual or diagram demonstrating their brilliance. In reality, few care about their methodology.[1]
2. *True nature*: This is the essence of who we are. True nature is not something we can acquire; it's something we discover. If we are self-aware, we regularly celebrate and express the positive aspects of ourselves. These may include serving others, being compassionate, demonstrating high integrity, being nonjudgmental, honest, and inclusive. Our shadow (or negative) character aspects are equally worth identifying and minimizing. They often show up as self-centeredness, false modesty, passive-aggressive behavior, gossiping, constantly evaluating others, being manipulative, dishonest, self-important, or self-doubting.

    Conner says "Cultivating character is about...leveraging not only what is already within us but recognizing it as the greatest asset we have as change practitioners...our true nature is our greatest asset. Only when we can stay centered on this and see it as core to the value we provide, will we be able to live up to our full potential and help others do the same."[2] Experiences, relationships, and circumstances may shift over time, but our true nature stays constant.
3. *Presence*: This is how we express our character and true nature to the world. I once confused presence with personality and physical appearance. While these contribute to how others perceive us, our character can only emerge when our presence is congruent with our true nature.

I often describe Tony Hsieh, the cofounder and CEO of Zappos, as someone with great character. He learned at an early age that his purpose is about serving customers and creating extraordinary social and professional experiences. When I met Tony, he came across as understated and reserved—until I asked him about Zappos' unique and somewhat obsessed customer-centric culture. Over the past decade, he and his team have created a billion dollar online enterprise that builds evangelical customer and employee communities. And yes, I'm one of their biggest customer evangelists.

In summary, Conner reminds us that "only when character and methodology interact synergistically can our heads and hearts merge to release the potential that is there.... Character differentiates our work much more than the tools we sometimes so jealously protect. This means that, as change practitioners, the secret sauce in our profession isn't in our heads, it's in our hearts."[3]

Once we have integrated our character with our technical abilities, we can enjoy living in the present moment because it becomes easier to accept and adapt to our current conditions. For example, we can recognize when we are leading an initiative that has a high probability of succeeding, and we can accept when a marketing initiative might fail in spite of our best efforts.

Strong character also fosters the self-confidence to recognize that many programs would otherwise flounder without our involvement. We don't take success or failure personally, nor do we fool ourselves into believing that we always like the outcome. In other words, we face the reality of the situation, learn from the experience and move forward.

Mindful marketers also anticipate some form of overt or covert resistance to our new ideas. Our ideas will, at some point, be overturned. If we constantly fight for our ideas, plans, and business models, we induce unnecessary suffering. Struggle will persist. Mindful marketers tell customers and stakeholders that our recommendations can either be embraced or rejected, and outline the benefits and pitfalls of each recommendation. It is not our goal to subject others to arm-twisting to win some fabricated "battle." Conner says it best: "Acceptance means to embrace something as a reality (even if an unwanted one) and incorporate it into the decision-making process regarding what to do next.... It's important that we share our observation if it appears clients *(or stakeholders)* are not operating in their own best interests (i.e., their current behavior will not give them what they say they want). However, to say or imply they are somehow "bad" or what they are doing is inherently wrong is not only inappropriate, it's generally ineffective."[4]

If you are a mindful marketing leader, you accept yourself, warts and all. You laugh at your blind spots and character defects. The greatest leaders I have met create their own ritual to foster acceptance and compassion for themselves, which naturally allows them to be more compassionate towards others. One example is Joseph Hoar, the U.S. General who served under Colin Powell in Somalia and the Middle East. While flying from New York to San Diego, I had the privilege of sitting next to him. He told me that every day, no matter what, he takes time to reflect.

2. *Aliveness.* This is the second quality of a mindful marketing leader. How often do you meet someone who has a physical glow? On most days, they express lightness about them. Their faces are radiant; their eyes alert. You may also notice that their voices are uplifting and animated. You find yourself wanting to spend more time with them than other people for no particular reason.

My friend and mentor, Cathy Hawk, refers to this type of person as someone who lives "lights on." Her work as the Founder of Clarity International© has greatly influenced my work over the past 12 years, and has helped me create a rewarding business and lifestyle. We will be referring to the Clarity Operating System™ in upcoming chapters.

Clarity International© provides a dialogue and inquiry framework to align one's vision with one's passion. Over twenty-two hundred CEOs, entrepreneurs, and leaders have enjoyed the benefits of Clarity. *Science of Mind* columnist Deborah Sandella described Clarity this way: "When people are enthusiastic about their lives, there is a noticeable change in the way they look and express.... The Hawks (Cathy and husband, Gary) suggest that all of us can live in this state of mind by consistently shifting our thinking from thoughts that drain energy to thoughts that enliven us."[5]

For me personally, living "lights on" means that my relationships with my clients, friends, and close family members are energetic and drama free. Clarity© has also taught me to rapidly notice when my thoughts and actions are draining and ineffective. I can rapidly recover from those patterns by shifting my thoughts, words, and actions in another direction. The Clarity Attention Guide™, shown in Figure 10–1, allows you to follow your energy and determine whether you are exhibiting "lights off" behaviors (which represent low-energy frequency) or "lights on" (or higher-energy frequency) behaviors.[6] Once you choose the latter, you begin to transition to living each day with more passion and purpose.

Figure 10.1 Clarity Attention Guide

CLARITY ATTENTION GUIDE AND BALANCE SHEET

EFFECTIVE
Solution Focused

	INDIVIDUALS What is my energy at work characterized by?	LEADERS Where is my energy focused as a leader?	
♦	Effortlessness	Service	♦
✳	High Noticing	Visionary	✳
●	Authenticity	Acknowledging	●
★	Dedication	Coaching	★
ⓒ	Enthusiasm	Modeling	ⓒ
⌘	Excitement	Confidence	⌘
■	Trust	Honesty	■
	Discomfort	Frustration	
■	Fear	Manipulating	■
⌘	Exhaustion	Sabotaging	⌘
ⓒ	Anxiety	Evaluating	ⓒ
★	Defiance	Telling	★
●	Self-Importance	Advising	●
✳	Habituation	Assuming	✳
♦	Overdoing	Dictatorial	♦

CHOICE POINT

THE TRANSITION LINE

EFFECTIVE
Flow

INEFFECTIVE
Problem Focused

INEFFECTIVE
Eddy

Copyright 2011, Clarity International; reprinted with permission.

I have found several applications for this Guide in day-to-day marketing activities and discussions. For example, in lieu of *dictating* the direction my clients want to take their marketing organization, I encourage them to ask, "What direction would best *serve* our customers?" There is a subtle difference between dictating outcomes and being a person of service. Dictating our wishes to others only works when we are facing a tragedy, turnaround, or emergency. Most marketing initiatives do not meet those conditions.

We will discuss other Clarity principles in Chapters 11 and 12 as we explore the role of energy and intention-setting on our decision-making and communications strategies.

3. *Articulateness.* An articulate marketing leader is a confident marketing leader. Possessing a broad vocabulary, and using it effectively

across all communications channels, can separate the persuasive from the passive.

In today's highly connected world, Twitter is a marketing leader's ally. Although social media is not a substitute for more substantial, personalized interactions with our teams, customers, and senior leadership teams, it has forced many of us to become more succinct and consistent with interactions across our online and offline channels.

An articulate marketer doesn't just recognize and instill the importance of great copywriting in her team. She also uses memorable storytelling and powerful language to convey her organization's vision across every communications channel. Author Brian Solis believes that "these new (online media) tools can bring people together and unite them under a common front or a concerted mission. At the center of any revolution is the desire to bring about change…it always comes down to people, shared experiences, and a common ambition." And it is people who need each other for leadership, support, and inspiration."[7]

4. *Aggregation.* A strategic marketing leader gains inspiration from unusual sources and actively seeks patterns across seemingly disparate platforms and places. I find my greatest inspiration and new ideas by spending time with people outside of my industry and by visiting new countries. When I spent a day touring Zappos, the innovative online retailer in Henderson, Nevada, I had no previous experience or understanding of online retailing. Yet I knew that Zappos' commitment to creating "wow" customer service experiences could inspire and inform my clients in other industries. Several of my business associates and clients have toured Zappos' facility and discovered several fresh service and marketing ideas for their own companies.

5. *Adaptability.* How quickly can you shift gears and go with the flow during times of rapid change? Being adaptable, and less rigid, is something that has taken me a couple of decades to embrace. I will never forget a conference I attended that featured the late Stephen Covey, a highly-acclaimed leadership expert and the author of *The 7 Habits of Highly Effective People*. I was told prior to the conference I would never get to schedule a live interview with Stephen due to his full schedule. While I felt disappointed, I was also surprised by what happened next.

At the last moment, the *Los Angeles Times* reporter cancelled, and an interview time slot opened. I had just seven minutes to prepare for a live meeting with Stephen! I faced a metaphorical fork in the road. I silently panicked and considered my options. Should I fake it and act as if I was prepared, or should I tell him I did not plan for this in advance?

I chose the latter option. When I told Stephen I was unprepared, he offered me an oatmeal cookie. We were off and running. It was the best 35-minute interview I can remember. I was proud of myself for living "in the moment."

Those are the five fundamentals of mindful leadership in today's chaotic world. Try on a few new behaviors. They will shed new light on how you interact with the world. As Marianne Williamson reminds us, "As we let our light shine, we unconsciously give other people permission to do the same. As we are liberated from our own fear, our presence actually liberates others."[8]

INNER MARKETING GURU Inquiry #10:

What mindful marketer quality am I willing to explore and practice today?

This page intentionally left blank

CHAPTER 11

PERSONAL ENERGY MANAGEMENT

Power is of two kinds. One is obtained by the fear of punishment and the other by acts of love. Power based on love is a thousand times more effective and permanent than the one derived from fear of punishment.

—Mahatma Gandhi

When we moved to the Washington, DC, suburbs in 2010, we started searching for a new home. One community fulfilled most of our wish list: it provided quiet, tree-lined streets, safe neighborhoods, mature landscaping, and large lots. That was the good news. The bad news was the mature trees, which reach one hundred feet tall or higher, creating a hazard when hurricanes hit the region. And hurricanes along the eastern seaboard can be brutal. In fact, our new neighborhood was notorious for tall trees falling on the above-ground power lines and causing power outages for up to five days.

With our having home offices, a five-day outage was not an option. We purchased a top-of-the-line generator to power the entire home.

Power outages don't just occur in our work and living spaces; they occur with our personal performance. You have probably met certain people who seem to operating on a low battery much of the time, their eyes half-shut, their voices without much of a tone of enthusiasm. You just want to reach across the table and offer them jumper cables.

In the United States, low energy and enthusiasm in the workforce have become standard operating procedure. *The Wall Street Journal* recently reported from a new Gallup poll that "52% of all full time workers in America are not involved in, enthusiastic about, or committed to their work. 18% are 'actively disengaged,' meaning they have gone beyond just checking out mentally, and could even be undermining colleagues' accomplishments. That leaves just 30% of American workers who feel excited about their jobs."[1]

If we believe Gallup's estimates, the impact of employing this high percentage of unhappy workers costs our country between $450 billion to $550 billion annually. The lack of engagement is expressed through high absenteeism and turnover, quality issues, and lost productivity."[2]

Western medical researchers are just beginning to discuss the mind-body connection in mainstream publications and established professional communities. It is no longer taboo to assert that energy-draining experiences and habits trigger physical and emotional distress at the individual, group, and global levels.

Some of these sources have developed peer-reviewed studies and findings, and others have developed performance toolkits that busy marketers can use in their daily lives.

In 2010, Doctors Barbara Frederickson and Bethany Kok at the University of North Carolina at Chapel Hill presented a study that suggests a direct correlation between our state of mind and biology. They observed that the vagus nerve, which originates in the brain and connects to many thoracic and abdominal organs, including the heart, sends "signals telling that organ to slow down during moments of calm and safety...healthy vagal function is reflected in a subtle increase in heart rate while breathing in and a subtle decrease while breathing out. The difference yields an index of vagal tone, and the value of this index is known to be connected with health. Low values are...linked to inflammation and heart attacks."[3]

When these psychologists experimented on 65 university staff for vagal tone, they observed that "vagal tone increased significantly in people who meditated, and hardly at all in those who did not...these findings suggest high vagal tone makes it easier to generate positive emotions and that this, in turn, drives vagal tone still higher."[4]

Dr. David Hawkins spent five decades exploring the mind-body connection until his passing in 2012. He authored eight books, including the bestseller *Power vs. Force* and *Orthomolecular Psychiatry*, which he coauthored with Nobel Laureate Linus Pauling. He coined the term "attractor fields" as a framework to help us reach peak performance in our lives.

Hawkins' view of how we manifest action and how events unfold was broader than Newtonian physics. In traditional Newtonian physics communities, events are believed to occur in a linear fashion, or sequentially (in other words, A causes B, which then causes C). In Hawkins' seminal book, *Power vs. Force: The Hidden Determinants of Human Behavior*, he accepts this theory, but considers it to be an oversimplification of how we operate in the world. Hawkins affirmed that aligning our thoughts with "attractor fields" is an effective approach to accomplishing peak performance.

In his book, he presents a personality scoring system that ranges from 0 to 1,000 (0 represents the lowest score, and 1,000 represents the highest level of consciousness and pure awareness). He created this system using applied kinesiology, or muscle testing.

Author and nurse Carla Thompson reported in 2012 that Hawkins' research revealed that "this kinesiologic response conveys man's capacity to differentiate not only positive from negative stimuli, but also anabolic from catabolic, and very dramatically, truth from falsity.... The research carried on for over 20 years to come up effectively with an anatomy of consciousness that reflects the entire human condition."[5]

Here are the energy levels outlined by David Hawkins:

- 20: Shame
- 30: Guilt
- 50: Apathy
- 75: Grief
- 100: Fear
- 125: Desire
- 150: Anger
- 175: Pride
- 200: Courage
- 250: Neutrality
- 310: Willingness
- 350: Acceptance
- 400: Reason
- 500: Love
- 540: Joy
- 600: Peace
- 700–1000: Enlightenment

According to the Personality-Development.org website, "For Hawkins, moving upward into higher states of consciousness is the only way to make meaningful progress in one's life. Sadly, the average individual only moves up 5 points in their entire lifetime. However, a focused effort to move into higher states can lead to incredible leaps of awareness in relatively short periods of time."[6]

Hawkins believed that two pivotal moments in our consciousness journey can lead us to high levels of awareness and performance. "There are two critical points that allow for major advancement. The first is at 200, the initial level of empowerment: Here, the willingness to stop blaming and accept responsibility for one's own actions, feelings, and beliefs arises—as long as cause and responsibility are projected outside of oneself, one will remain in the powerless mode of victimhood."

The second pivot point happens at the 500 level, "which is reached by accepting love and nonjudgmental forgiveness as a lifestyle, exercising unconditional kindness to all persons, things, and events *without exception*."[7] He also stated that "Any meaningful human satisfaction cannot commence until the level of 250, where some degree of self-confidence begins to emerge as a basis for positive life experiences in the evolution of consciousness."[8]

For 20 years, Cathy and Gary Hawk of Clarity International have been teaching leaders how to shift our thinking from thoughts that drain energy (which typically fall below 250 points on Hawkins' personality scale) to thoughts that energize us (which are thoughts that represent 250 points or higher on the scale).

The Hawks remind us that "Holding your own personal energy steadily and not letting yourself become drained or frenetic is the key to creating a vibrant life. To help maintain your positive energy in all that you do, recognize that there are three distinct energy fields that you are in touch with at all times":[9]

Personal Field (also known as the Human Energy System)—The Hawks describe this as an invisible bubble that follows us and "contains your mind and your thoughts, your body, your health, your spirit and your creativity."[10] Thankfully, we can directly shift the strength of our personal field through our choices. We can choose our thoughts, our lifestyle, our sleep habits, our language, and our diet.

We previously discussed the power of the spoken and written word, which is a reflection of our character. Our language directly fuels, or drains, our personal field. One language distinction that I often hear in some organizations permeates marketing copy. Some companies clearly write lights-off ads about "defeating Company X" and "killing the competition." Lights-on marketing copy focuses more on an improved condition for the target customer or on painting a picture of a better future. Apple co-founder, Steve Jobs, did this brilliantly. He imagined new product ideas well before customers knew they wanted or needed them. Patagonia's mission statements serves as another example of lights-on language: "Build the best product, cause no unnecessary harm, use business to inspire and implement solutions to the environmental crisis."[11] Patagonia founder Yvon Chouinard's 40-year commitment to the great outdoors and to stewardship of our limited and precious natural resources is reflected in this statement.

The Near Field (also known as the Environmental Energy System)—equates to your immediate surroundings, which include your home, friendships, family, neighborhood, work setting, and community. You cannot control this field; however, you can influence it. When my parents advised me to choose my husband and my friends wisely, they were right. I chose to walk away from a high-paying corporate position because my values did not align with the culture of the founders. The Hawks suggest we ask three questions to keep our near field optimized:

- "Does my environment enhance my life?
- Do I feel soothed when I walk into my home or office?
- Do my friends, partners, and neighbors support me?"[12]

Mindful marketers accept that they cannot always change an energy-draining, listless work environment without leaving for a new position. Instead of complaining, blaming, or playing the victim, they seek out a new opportunity.

It's essential to create "unplugged moments" in our near field. We mentioned that the two biggest saboteurs to staying focused and balanced are distractions and interruptions. Turning off technology distractions allows our brain to process new ideas, digest the daily events, and empty the metaphorical filing cabinet in our brain, which is also called the Reticular Activation System (RAS). Great things can happen when we turn off these devices, even for just 30 minutes per day.

Massachusetts Institute of Technology professor and bestselling author Sherry Turkle reminds us of the impact of excessive use of technology within our work settings and personal surroundings. "Technology has a paradoxical effect—it can make you MORE lonely, and if you don't teach your children to be alone, they will feel lonely."[13] Her comments may sound contradictory, but they aren't. Look at the people who hide behind a social media platform and sacrifice human interaction for digital diatribe.

The Remote Field (also known as the Distant Energy System)—includes economic forces, wars, political conflict, natural disasters, and social strife. While we may influence these events and conditions through philanthropic means, we cannot change them.

In my younger years, I was easily seduced (and sometimes enveloped) by the remote field. I spent countless months reflecting on the seemingly infinite tragedies that occurred on September 11, 2001. That was how I operated prior to understanding these energy fields. I found myself being consumed by the heaviness and sadness of those days, unable to focus on my own work and family.

Media outlets and academic circles encourage us to focus on the remote field from our days in grammar school through our college years. We are rewarded for our understanding of geography, politics, science, social studies, and global affairs. The Hawks see this imbalance as physically and emotionally detrimental. "The daily news bombards us with information about wars and conflicts, the ups and downs of the economy, crime, natural catastrophes, and global tragedies.... When you let negativity in this field consume you, and you worry about events you cannot control, you can easily lose your own energy."[14]

Mindful marketers need to create systems to mitigate the remote field forces. These approaches work well for me:

1. *Carefully manage my media exposure.* I shut down news programs and online channels where the commentators are yelling and berating one another or delving into polarizing political topics. I also avoid watching late night news because it disrupts my sleep.
2. *Listen to inspiring business leaders and positive media outlets.* These programs typically contain moderate voice tones and points of view versus radical, accusatory ones.
3. *Design marketing content that creates new possibilities and an empowering vision for stakeholders.* Avoid themes that focus on killing the competition or outwardly berating your rivals.

In the next chapter, you will find 16 language distinctions, shown in Figure 12–2, to incorporate into your content.

4. *Read publications that represent what the Hawks refer to as "balanced coverage."*[15] While I appreciate the extensive global business coverage that *The Wall Street Journal* provides, I am aware that its relatively new owners (the Murdoch family) make its highly conservative political views drive most of the content. I balance my time reading that publication with *The Economist*, *Entrepreneur*, and *FastCompany* (which laud entrepreneurship, innovation, and socially conscious businesses).

Is your professional and personal potential dependent on your ability to develop, express, and sustain optimal levels of energy? Absolutely. Can you minimize your exposure to energy-sucking environments? With practice, you can.

Follow these strategies to model "lights-on" behavior with other marketers:

1. Acknowledge your physical reactions to low-energy, draining situations. Your mindfulness practice will help you quickly dial into those reactions and identify them at a physical level. Self-medicating through drugs, sleep deprivation, gambling, excessive shopping, alcohol, or other self-defeating habits only provide temporary succor.
2. Choose what happens next. How will you react to those persistent conditions within each of the three fields? Will you choose to learn from them and change your personal and near fields, or complain and be victimized by them?
3. Release your grip on the situation. When I compete in open water swims, I will sometimes register for a series of races over a long weekend. Sometimes I don't achieve my registered race times, and I become disappointed. I quietly express my frustration to my husband, identify the causes, change into a dry swimsuit, and prepare for the next race. That's my ritual. That race is done. I cannot repeat it. Why can't we do the same with a failed marketing campaign?
4. Focus on serving others. Bestselling author Tony Schwartz reminds us that "one of the best ways to make yourself feel better is to make someone else feel better... people who give

without expecting anything in return actually turn out not only to feel better for having done so, but also to be more successful.... Giving...does not require extraordinary acts of sacrifice. It simply involves a focus on acting in the interests of others. When takers succeed, there is usually someone else who loses. When givers give, it spreads and cascades."[16]

> **INNER MARKETING GURU Inquiry #11:**
>
> What can I do right now to optimize my personal and near energy fields, and reach new levels of performance?

CHAPTER 12

THE POWER OF PRESENT MOMENT LANGUAGE

Who you're being is so loud I cannot hear what you're saying.
—Ralph Waldo Emerson

In a previous chapter I outlined the importance of being an articulate mindful marketer. An articulate marketing leader is a confident marketing leader. While language sets the persuasive apart from the passive, being articulate requires more skills than exhibiting a strong command of language. I believe that being aware of our surroundings and being intentional are just as important as being linguistically fluent.

First, let's explore how articulate marketers fulfill a very broad mission for their organization. They create excitement for and commitment to the company's vision; they also fulfill a customer's unmet needs, create new opportunities where they previously did not exist, and develop messages (often known as "proof points") to demonstrate the value of doing business with their organization. That isn't news to seasoned marketers. An often-overlooked reader or customer benefit is the degree to which articulate messages can reduce anxiety for the listener. And in today's business world, we could use a smaller dose of anxiety-laden messages. As we have discussed in Section 1, mistrust of authority, accountability standards, and uncertainty have reached peak levels.

No matter how many scenarios we anticipate and build into our crisis plan, mishaps, misdeeds, and management fiascos can still knock us off our talking points. Some events are simply out of our control.

In my career, I have lost a handful of sales opportunities because the prospective client was suddenly acquired, and all new investments were halted. I initially felt devastated. One of my friends, who is the CEO of a $50M information technology (IT) consulting firm, watched 30 percent of their revenues evaporate overnight due to the 2013 U.S. government shutdown. These are just two examples of unplanned calamities. Government shutdowns, mergers, a sudden ethical breach, or employee defection can also happen. Being present to the situation and recognizing what part we can influence or control enables us to prepare a more empowering response. Our response to those events can make a difference between recovery and despair.

Chip Conley, founder of Joie de Vivre Hotels and two-time bestselling author, was inspired to write *Emotional Equations* in response to the hospitality industry downturn during the Great Recession. The equations he developed helped him and his employees adapt to the new market dynamics. He believes that "anxiety is the most prevalent emotion in most organizations in the United States today.... Anxiety has two component parts: it's what you don't know and what you can't control. So anxiety...equals uncertainty times powerlessness." [1]

We cannot eliminate uncertainty, but we can manage our anxiety levels. When we face a crisis or are preparing for an important meeting, we can pause and ask, "What information do we know is true, and how can we influence or act on that?"

Once we know what we can influence, it becomes much easier to be intentional. Being intentional overshadows and guides communications strategy, and is something that most marketing seminars and educational programs omit. Intentionality is defined as *the process of aligning our attitude, thoughts and actions, both conscious and unconscious, to directly influence a situation or experience.*

Being intentional does not mean we want to control the outcomes or follow some recipe for success. *FastCompany* contributor Drake Baer describes the power of intention beautifully: "Success is nonlinear: we can't know how something will turn out at its outset. Not even Google can predict how employees will perform at the point of hire. As David Lee observes, the savviest entrepreneurs cooperate with the unpredictability: when Jeff Bezos is talking about going down 'blind alleys' that turn into 'broad avenues,' he's really talking about exploring unproven trajectories can yield [sic] high-flying business. You could say that Bezos is lucky, but it might be more accurate to say that he's cooperating with chance."[2] I take Baer's concept one step further. I believe that Google leadership and Bezos are examples of intentional marketers.

Once we have become clear on what areas we can control or influence, we can carve a path to climb the "Persuasion Pyramid." I borrowed this process from Alan Weiss,[3] and created a visual to show the evolution of effective communication, shown in Figure 12.1. With practice, the mindful marketer has the ability to navigate through this Persuasion Pyramid with ease.

Here's how marketers can use this pyramid on a daily basis. Begin by generating interest with a better way of doing things—perhaps you are introducing a brand new solution or product that your customers never imagined. Netflix introduced a new way of experiencing entertainment and disrupted Blockbuster into bankruptcy. Apple accomplished this when they introduced the first iPad, which empowers us to manage a multitude of tasks without being chained to a traditional laptop or desktop computer.

This first step in climbing the pyramid is not based solely on understanding a customer's needs at an intellectual level. This step must also reflect a sense of empathy for the customer's situation. Many marketing researchers and strategists miss this point entirely. While many marketers excel at *cognitive empathy*, or understanding another person's

Figure 12.1 The Persuasion Pyramid

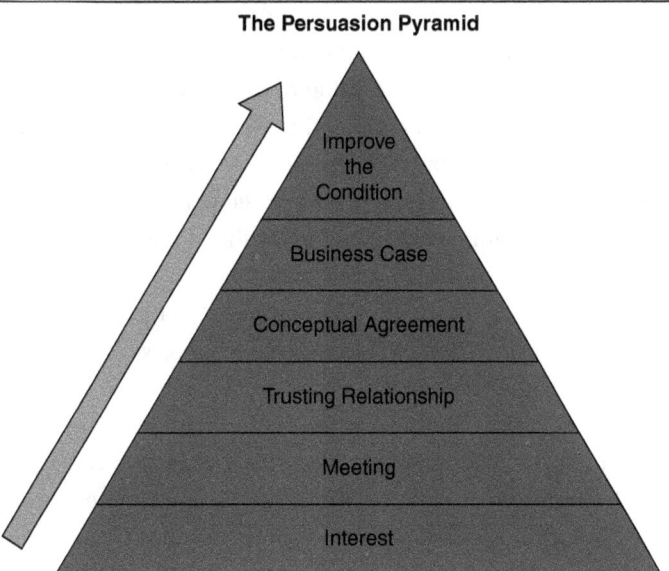

Copyright 2012, Alan Weiss. All rights reserved.

perspective, some forget to incorporate *affective empathy*, or the response to someone's emotional state, into their marketing messaging and branding activity.

According to Douglas Van Praet, author of *Unconscious Branding: How Neuroscience can Empower (and Inspire) Marketing*, "marketers need to understand and personally experience two types of empathy: *affective empathy* and *cognitive empathy*." The interest-creation stage starts with building rapport, and building rapport begins with evoking an emotional reaction in response to the other person or audience."[4] Without both aspects of empathy, a marketer can tumble into what Van Praet calls the "Dark Triad" personality vortex: narcissism, Machiavellianism, and psychopathy. None of these behaviors befit a mindful marketer.

Interest facilitates meetings, either live or virtual. Meetings are essential to building trusting relationships. Trusting relationships, in turn, establish permission from the other person to build conceptual agreement. You know you have reached a solid trust level when the other person turns to you, unsolicited, for advice, or shares confidential information with you.

Conceptual agreement, a term coined by Weiss in his seminal book, *Million Dollar Consulting*, is consummated when three conditions are met: first, when your buyer or customer agrees to a set of objectives, second, when you clearly understand their measures of success (personal success measures or key performance indicators), and third, when they are clear and excited about the value of working with you. They must see value from several perspectives: value to them personally, value to their customers, value to investors, and value to other internal stakeholders. This conversation can happen in as little as ten minutes in a retail interaction, such as when a salesperson interacts with a customer. In buying conversations for complex, expensive business solutions, this conversation could be completed in a one-hour meeting, or it could require three. Much depends on the level of complexity of the solution and the number of key stakeholders and beneficiaries involved.

Conceptual agreement between buyer and seller, or between peers, is essential because it fuels your business case. Gaining support for your business case ultimately enables you to improve the financial or emotional condition of your customers, which ultimately enables you to improve your organization's condition. If you don't know what condition or scenario they want to improve or transform, you are relegated to their growing pile of distractions.

This persuasion process is ostensibly rudimentary. Yet you would be surprised at how many people skip the first few stages and dive into conceptual agreement conversations. I subscribe to a newsletter from a publicly traded software company that publishes monthly customer success stories. Their publication helps me stay abreast of the trends in their industry. Their information falls flat for several reasons: they are assuming that a) I fit their customer profile; b) I am evaluating some kind of solution that they provide; and c) I have budget to invest in their solution. Their messaging is ideally targeted toward companies that already plan on evaluating their type of solution—yet is being scattered across their entire subscriber base. If I were to advise their CMO, I would recommend that he avoid sending these mass emails to every subscriber and only focus on those who are actively evaluating their solution.

Vocabulary plays a pivotal role in three scenarios: when you are setting your intentions, when you are constructing a message, and when you are navigating the pyramid. The right words build trust and set the tone, or energy level, for every conversation. This, in turn, gives us permission to shepherd others in a meaningful, positive direction.

Every word has its own meaning to the reader. Some are positive, and some are negative. In the marketing profession, language has been used and abused. Steve Yastrow, author of *We: The Ideal Customer Relationship*, presents some excellent contrasts between marketing terminology that is rooted in sports and military metaphors, and inspiring, metaphor-free language. He also encourages us to stop using targeting terminology. For example, these are three of his least favorite comments from marketers:

- "We're attacking the target market with a rifle shot approach."
- "We're in a fierce battle with the competition to capture market share."
- "We've scheduled a volley of advertising for the fall."[5]

These comments and allusions to war and sports continue to build barriers—or an "us versus them" mentality between customers and marketers. Yastrow asks, "If I want to persuade you of something, would I have much luck if I tried to 'capture' or 'target' you?"[6]

Mindful marketers can break down these linguistic barricades by replacing their old vocabulary. Tables 12.1 shows a few possibilities to consider.

Table 12.1 The Marketing Language Meter™

Low-energy marketing language	*High-energy* marketing language
target	serve
imitate	innovate or manifest
pitch	converse or acknowledge
push	shepherd
chase	earn or connect
attack	engage or participate
pursue	nurture
penetrate	expand
exploit	invite
saturate	grow
capture	engage or connect
seduce	engage or excite
manipulate	dance
tell	guide
compete	collaborate
revenue stream	legacy or impact

Copyright 2014, Lisa Nirell. All rights reserved.

Customer engagement, which begins with intentionality, is not a new idea. Yet few companies have reached customer engagement nirvana. This happens when referrals appear serendipitously and online marketing and demand happen consistently and predictably with minimal effort or tweaking. Much like weight loss, smoking cessation, and learning a new sport, human engagement and ongoing conversation require practice. And practice happens more effortlessly when we create new rituals.

Here are four rituals that will help you fuel trusting and lasting relationships:

1. *Commit time to staying future focused.* In Western society, it is not uncommon to lead conversations with what isn't working and to get caught up in the minutiae of today's problems. In fact, many marketing executives in my community have told me that they are either operating in problem-solving or decision-making mode. Problem solving concentrates on fixing persistent issues that surfaced sometime in the past, while decision-making fixes tactical, daily dilemmas. Innovators, on the other hand, create time to ask, "What's next?" and

"How can we create a breakthrough, or make this easier for our customers tomorrow?"

2. *Incorporate metaphors into your conversation.* The other day, I was speaking with the VP of Marketing of a $600M technology firm. He wanted to arrange a retainer for my advisory services. He had just accepted a new role at a well-established company, and he was hired to reinvigorate their market position and brand. They had less than 18 months to gain first-mover advantage in the Customer Relationship Management (CRM) and customer service arenas.

I explained to him that hiring me is akin to scheduling a building inspection with a fire marshal. A marshal can help your organization prevent a tragic building fire by recommending proactive safety measures, such as posting "No Smoking" signs and safe paths of egress. Reorganizing his current marketing team and reallocating budgetary items based solely on his previous personal career experiences would prove to be a recipe for costly surprises down the road, such as attrition of his best team members and an uncooperative board. Skipping the inspection could force him to call the fire station. This metaphorical distinction made it easy for him to quickly recognize my value.

3. *Establish the Check-In Process™ with your team or customers.*

Clarity Founder Cathy Hawk created a Check-In Process© to help leaders stay present, set their intentions, and establish a positive tone for any conversation or meeting. Long term, this exercise refines our ability to observe, which contributes to greater mindfulness and present moment awareness.

THE CHECK-IN PROCESS©

When I begin my CMO peer group gatherings, I follow these basic Check-In Process© steps:

What's different since our last meeting?

State one thing that they have noticed that's different in their personal or near field.

What worked and what didn't work in your performance?

State one thing that worked in the past few days or weeks, and one thing that didn't work. The key point is to remove all judgment, blame, or emotional attachment to the situation.

What is the current state of my mind, body, and spirit?

Mindfulness is heightened when we can identify changes in our physical and emotional states. They may mention states such as tired, excited, relieved, optimistic, etc.

What are you grateful for?

Expressing gratitude shifts our focus away from what we don't have (future focused) to what makes us happy (present focused). One Seventh Generation blogger says that "instead of dwelling on what we don't have, or what we want, (gratitude helps us) focus on areas where we already feel fulfilled. Practicing shifting our focus can feel a bit forced at first—but you can practice gratitude to get better at living with it—and to be happier overall."[7]

What is your intention for the meeting/day/week?

Unlike concrete, measurable goals, an intention is a state of being that will facilitate a positive outcome. For example, "my intentions are to stay focused on my top priorities today and to create time for exercise."[8]

Jason Lake, CEO of Eyecare Specialties in central Missouri, uses this process to avert employee and patient emergencies and misunderstandings. "At the beginning of our office meetings, we spend 10 minutes to express gratitude. This positive energy will dictate how the day will unfold at that office location. We also have MOM meeting [Morning Opportunity Meeting] to discuss 'what went right yesterday?' We spend a lot of time talking about what is working."

Lake and his team have much to celebrate. "We track several metrics on a monthly basis for each doctor. Along with our regular surveys and open book management, we can quickly

see if our culture is thriving." Today, Eyecare Specialties ranks in the top 2 percent among their peer group for profitability, and is rated one of the top-10 optometrists in Missouri.[9]
4. *Create and monitor listening posts:* Listening to team members and customer conversations in reputable online and offline forums will alert you to new trends and troubles. Top marketers create open forums with the intention of encouraging honest dialogue and avoiding excessive monitoring or editing to manipulate the conversations. The marketing team led by John Morris, senior director of the SAP Business One Marketing team, creates positioning and demand strategies for SAP's business management software for small- to mid-sized companies. "In the past, I was involved with the SAP Community Network (SCN), the social network for all SAP professionals. Today, SAP has over 2.5 million participants. We use this as a listening post for Business One and a place to announce new features."[10]

An articulate marketer exudes honesty because they regularly express and celebrate their true nature. Customers and peers, in turn, recognize and reward that honesty at a visceral level. Bryant Jaquez, cofounder of media buying agency Noble Creative, made this a core precept when he launched the firm. "We don't want our employees to devote invaluable neural mechanisms on pretending to be someone else. We have found that people are happier and more effective when they are allowed to be themselves. This approach gives people the freedom to be transparent, which is actually an aid in most creative processes. Additionally, our company has a stronger sense of teamwork because they feel genuinely cared about by their co-workers."[11]

It's not what you say that matters; it's what people hear. Our intentions, coupled with "present moment language," ignite thoughtful discussions and revolutionary thinking.

INNER MARKETING GURU Inquiry #12:

What scenarios am I facing where I can practice present moment language and techniques?

This page intentionally left blank

CHAPTER 13

MINDFUL PLANNING AND DECISION-MAKING

Many are destined to reason wrongly; others, not to reason at all; and others to persecute those who do reason.
—Voltaire

I'm a food snob. There, I said it.

I shun packaged produce, and feel a deep sadness when our garden withers in the fall. Picking berries and greens and buying fresh, local produce have been joyful yet temporary pleasures from the time I was a young girl. My dad used to grow rhubarb and cucumbers, which my grandmother would magically turn into strawberry rhubarb preserves and sweet pickles. Those canned items would officially mark the end of summer, and they delighted us throughout the darker months. (What a perfect example of impermanence, a cornerstone Buddhist principle!)

If mindfulness represents the fresh ingredients in our marketing leadership recipe, then critical thinking is the Mason jar. One cannot exist without the other. That is why a solid foundation in critical thinking provides marketers with the discipline and grounding for career longevity.

When I work with clients to resolve complex dilemmas, I listen for their critical thinking abilities. A critical thinker is someone who has an appreciation and understanding of the complexities in our world and can navigate through them. They also have other qualities in common:

1. They are naturally curious about the world around them
2. They make time to form a perspective on complex issues or challenges

3. They can formulate their own insights and judgment without relying on an authoritative figure to do the thinking for them
4. They take an interest in topics that are, on the surface, completely unrelated to their line of work. Consequently, they often discover patterns and themes across seemingly disparate topics.
5. They engage in constructive, not destructive, criticism. In other words, they avoid tearing down someone else's way of thinking or publicly attacking their character for personal gain.
6. They ask for evidence to help them assess the severity of a situation and to formulate a decision.
7. They are aware of their personal "global goggles," which are perspectives that we have acquired in our earlier years. These perspectives shape our worldview. Critical thinkers are willing to question and suspend them.

These seven qualities don't come easy, and for most people, it can take years, if not decades, to reach the critical thinking state. John Chaffee, professor of philosophy at La Guardia College, created a three-part, condensed version of a human thought model, which was inspired by Harvard psychologist William Perry. Chaffee's seminal book on *The Thinker's Way* outlines his three-stage model, which succinctly traces how we evolve from one stage of thinking to the next.

According to Chaffee, "People in Stage 1, *The Garden of Eden* stage of thinking, tend to see the world in black and white, right and wrong. How do they determine what is right, what to believe? The 'authorities' tell them. Just as in the biblical Garden of Eden, knowledge is absolute and unchanging, but it is in the sole possession of the authorities…ordinary people…must rely on the experts…there is no possibility of compromise or negotiation…. The first authorities we encounter are usually our parents."[1]

The pristine paradise of ponderment suddenly shatters when the Garden of Eden thinker realizes that authorities disagree with each other, and it is no longer clear whom they can truly believe. That sudden epiphany, combined with the strong desire to be open to new ideas and the intellectual firepower to review multiple perspectives, transforms the Garden of Eden thinker into the next stage: *Anything Goes.*

Chaffee reasons that an Anything Goes thinker "has rejected the dogmatic, authoritarian framework of Stage 1."[2] That's the encouraging news. The bad news is that, for a time, the Anything Goes thinker will believe that one point of view is no better than another. Let sleeping dogs lie; let everyone defend their point of view; there's room for every perspective. The multitude of opinions regarding politics, religion, science, morality, business modeling, branding, health and fitness, and other topics are simply, as Chaffee says, "matters of taste." [3] The flaw in this belief is that we will never feel inclined to view certain acts or beliefs as heinous (such as animal abuse and race discrimination), nor to applaud acts worth rewarding (such as saving a life, winning a marathon, or blowing the whistle on a company that abuses factory workers).

Stage 3, *The Critical Thinker*, synthesizes *Anything Goes* and *Garden of Eden* thinking. Chaffee defines this brilliantly: "When people achieve this level of understanding, they recognize that some viewpoints are better than other viewpoints, not simply because authorities say so, but because there are compelling reasons to support these viewpoints. At the same time, people in this stage are open-minded toward other viewpoints, especially those that disagree with theirs."[4] A seasoned Critical Thinker allows their views to sink in and evolve over time, and regularly listens to new perspectives. They are also flexible and, when compelled, will change their position on a topic. Don't confuse this with being a perpetual flip-flopper, a common trait among some politicians who lead by following poll numbers, or business leaders who avoid making tough decisions due to fear of damaging friendships with their direct reports.

Stage 3 critical thinking is an essential ingredient for developing an effective marketing plan and optimizing your role as a marketing leader. Yet you would be surprised at the number of highly intelligent marketing executives who work at viable, fast-growth companies and operate without using any marketing plan. Some blame this on a lack of time; others simply prefer to "wing it."

In my experience, running a marketing organization without a marketing plan is an unintentional (versus intentional) act. It represents doing the same things in the new year and expecting the same results. It's the antithesis of being intentional or innovative. How would a company operate if the chief financial officer, VP of Manufacturing, and chief operating officer functioned this way? Sheer chaos would rule. Without a written marketing plan, it becomes increasingly difficult to demonstrate how you gathered information, how you formed your opinions, and what disparate sources you used to formulate recommendations. In other words, you'll probably be stuck at Level 2 thinking.

Being a Level 3 thinker requires you to design the right conditions for your ideas and plans to thrive. That's why I believe in *creating the environment* for your plan to succeed before you write the plan. This will enable you to develop a simple plan that you can share and communicate to others—especially those who may not fully understand the role and long-term value of marketing. These seven steps will move you in the right direction:

1. *Ask questions, even if you don't like the answers.* When was the last time you interviewed customers, team members, and executives to establish a baseline of your organization's current state? While this process is essential for anyone who joins a new organization, it's also highly effective for others who notice significant market or cultural shifts within their companies. Consider using this holistic framework, the **Performance Accelerant Model (PAM)**™, for your fact-finding (see Figure 13.1). I created this tool to help my clients immediately influence and impact their organization. It can be especially valuable for newly promoted or appointed executives.
2. *Rehearse how you will communicate your vision.* Can you explain your *current state of business* and *future desired state* in front of other people with your eyes closed? What is your physical reaction when you state your future vision out loud? Your visceral response will give you an early indication (or a warning signal) of how your message will land with others.
3. *Get creative on how you hire the right people to do new jobs.* Today, marketing leaders are expected to hire data scientists, content marketing experts, and online marketing gurus. Many of these positions didn't exist three years ago. Join forces with your CMO peer group, local universities, and scientific associations to find out what knowledge, skills, and abilities they are using to define and recruit for these pivotal positions.
4. *Write the plan.* Your colleagues are intelligent, but they are not mind readers. Unless we write down our plans, our brains have no way of recording and filtering that information. The Reticular Activation System, or RAS for short, is a function

Figure 13.1 Performance Accelerator Model

Performance Accelerator Model™

Internal Team

1. What have been your best experiences here? *What* makes us successful?
2. *What* makes us successful in the marketplace? *Who* makes us successful?
3. How do things really get done in this organization?
4. Where do you spend most of your time: innovating, or problem-solving?
5. How are people rewarded and recognized: individually, or as teams? What is the ratio?
6. What can I do to help you be more effective at your job?
7. What ideas do you have for growing the company?

Executives

1. Where would you like to see the company in 1–2 years?
2. What makes us successful in marketplace? Who makes us successful?
3. What percentage of your time do you spend innovating versus problem-solving?
4. What KPIs do you show the Board? Where do continuous innovation and customer satisfaction fit into these KPIs?
5. What other companies do you admire, and why? (not restricted to our industry)
6. What ideas do you have for growing the company?

Customers

1. What have been your best experiences here? Who was involved?
2. What made you choose our company?
3. How are you better off from working with us?
4. Historically, how rapidly have we responded to your changing needs? Examples?
5. What makes us stand out in the industry? (listening for values and brand themes)
6. How familiar are you with our company's values?
7. If you had three wishes for doing business with our company, what would they be?

Culture

1. Who are the "go to" people that get things done informally?
2. What are some new technologies or programs that I never had a chance to implement in the past, or in my previous role?
3. What are the stated values, and what are the operating values? How large is the gap between the two?
4. What percentage of my team can consistently and correctly explain what we do?
5. To what degree are equality and diversity encouraged in our hiring, team development and retention programs?
6. What aspects of my leadership style will work here? What aspects do I need to stop doing?

Copyright 2014, Lisa Nirell. All rights reserved.

of our brain, which performs this function for us. Executing any plan without a written guide leads to insane practices, such as one client of mine whose CEO announced 21 high-priority initiatives for 2013.

5. *Create the structure to succeed.* This doesn't refer only to your organization's structure. It also includes how you structure your *life*. Do you have your refrigerator stocked with healthy foods to fuel your week? Have you delegated all nonessential tasks to experts, such as housekeepers, bookkeepers, and pet sitters? Is your home set up for peaceful sleep? Every hour counts. One of my clients once ran a $5M technology consultancy, and was still doing her own bookkeeping when we began working together—until she realized someone could perform that function much more quickly, and for a fraction of her billable fee.

6. *Create a balanced plan that blends past, present, and future thinking.* If your marketing department is strictly operating like a marketing drive-through window, you are probably spending over 80 percent of your time either fixing yesterday's persistent, chronic problems, or making decisions about today's ad-hoc issues and opportunities. That leaves you less than 20 percent of your day to innovate and ponder the future. If you were hired to be a firefighter, and not a fire marshal, rethink your role and your true long-term value at that company.

7. *Develop courage, and be willing to get fired.* I saw Jeffrey Hayzlett deliver a dynamic keynote session at a major marketing conference in 2012. He shared a story that still makes me chuckle. While he was the CMO at Kodak, he was hired to resurrect their stodgy brand and create new ideas to help with their turnaround. One detail that annoyed him was the employee name badges. The employees' photos were seriously outdated. This was not a positive reflection on a company who prided themselves on their photographic prowess.

One day, he teamed up with an information technology colleague in the data center and removed all of the outdated employee photos from the servers. He sidestepped authority, and human resources was incensed. He didn't care whether he got fired or not; he simply could not allow this obvious brand violation to continue.

HOW MIRAVAL RESORT'S CMO FOSTERS PRESENT-MOMENT AWARENESS AND CRITICAL THINKING

I spoke with Carol Stratford, the former VP of Marketing, Reservations and Revenue Management for Miraval Resort and Spa. This world-class resort is tucked away in Tucson, Arizona, and employs 300 full-time team members. Miraval was designed to foster mindful, healthy lifestyles. They offer a variety of wellness, yoga, and fitness programs, as well as private sessions. Today, 30 percent of their guests are repeat customers.

Stratford joined the Resort in 2011 until 2014. She relocated from a high-profile East Coast marketing role to a resort setting in the bucolic foothills of the Santa Catalina Mountains. We explored the mindfulness strategies she practices with her team, and the positive results they have created. Below are excerpts from our conversation.

1. Describe the size and scope of your team and marketing responsibilities.

I have 3 marketing professionals on my team, 13 reservation agents, and a number of agencies handling our digital, creative, public relations, and other functions.

2. How do you integrate mindfulness into your marketing organization?

Mindfulness is part of our marketing message: "Guests come to Miraval individually or with family and friends to relax, refresh, and to learn to live and feel better. There are no strict regimens. Instead, choice is the guiding principle, with a wide range of programs and experiences designed to create overall well-being and help guests become more aware of themselves and their surroundings. They learn to live in the moment through means that work best for them."

3. How did you adapt to the Miraval culture, and how did it inform your decisions?

"In my first two weeks, I never went to my office. Instead, I participated in 60 percent of the Miraval programs before I even started working in my office. As soon as I officially started, I encouraged my team to leave on time. During our meetings, we put away our iPhones. Over time, I also taught my team to constantly ask: '*What's on the horizon?*'"

4. Where else does mindfulness play a role in decision-making?

"When I first arrived, I noticed a lot of my team members were bogged down in things that don't really drive the business. I tried to refocus their efforts. For example, we redesigned the entire website. I gave this task to one person who was excited to learn more about online marketing. I noticed another person was excellent at managing details. I changed what she was doing so that she handles PR. She also organizes our photo shoots. I also encouraged people to say NO to things."

I also teach them by example. For instance, I call them into the office and tell them a dilemma that I'm facing. I ask them how they would handle that given situation. As time goes on, my team is questioning my choices more often. That shows they are thinking more strategically. Now we spend time talking about things such as our new creative campaign, our latest brand guidebook, our style guide, our new website, and the goals for promoting our new resort property that we're building in Somerset County, New Jersey."

"I also encourage people to go with their gut because we know the guests. We use data mining as a way to get the conversation going. Some of the nuances of things happening at the resort do not show up in the reports. We try to incorporate what's going on with the property. Analytics and reports don't totally drive everything."

"Being mindful makes our team pause and think. A lot of times, people just react, and your answers may not be as effective and strategic. Forty percent of my team uses Miraval on a regular basis. I take one of my team members every week, and we walk around the property. We are able to discuss things we might not do in an office setting. As a marketing team we owe it to ourselves to try new programs and services, lectures, and classes."

5. Conflict is natural when you implement change, and often encouraged during critical thinking discussions. How did you handle conflict when you joined the company?

"I made a lot of changes when I arrived in the first year. I tried to be respectful, and I listened to people. I wanted to understand where the resistance was coming from. I educated them on the future vision to the best of my ability. Some stayed; others moved on."

6. Two years after joining Miraval, what results are you experiencing?

"This will be one of our most successful years. We are celebrating 8 out of the past 12 months as record months in the history of the resort in terms of revenue and occupancy.

In addition, we recently won an innovative award from iSpa for MyMiraval.com. This is an online personality tool that our guests can take before they arrive. Their responses indicate what activities they should do, which are determined by their current lifestyle. They then speak to one of our coordinators to help them make the most of their stay. This really helps us, because we offer over one hundred treatments and programs. About 80 percent of our guests take the test. Our activities coordinators can be much more effective on the phone with the guest, and it allows us to offer a much more personalized guest experience."

7. What advice and strategies would you offer marketing leaders who are just getting started on the path to mindfulness?

We are so fast paced that we don't allow ourselves the time to reflect. Find five minutes where you can just "be." Think about the day before it unfolds. This ritual has made me a better person all around. Everybody can find five minutes!

Plan big things and meetings in the morning, such as strategy sessions and interviews.

> Work on things that require less brain power in the afternoon. Stratford summarized our conversation with this timely reminder: "You give so much to the company that you need to make time for yourself."[5]

Mindful planning is a great way to enjoy the fruits of your labor throughout the year, and alleviate many common pesky weeds and insects.

INNER MARKETING GURU Inquiry #13:

How can the Performance Accelerant Model™ raise my awareness and improve my critical thinking abilities?

CHAPTER 14

DESIGNING WITH INTENTION

What's the good of a house if you don't have a good planet to put it on?

—Henry David Thoreau

The history of sustainable architecture and design provides some insights on how today's mindful work settings have evolved. The roots of sustainable design are both informative and inspiring. It's worthwhile to review how these relatively modern design precepts can guide mindful marketers toward greater harmony, satisfaction, and productivity.

Today's sustainable design luminaries recognized that creating the most innovative building without considering the long-term implications for future generations created a zero-sum, unfulfilling game. William McDonough, the creator of the *Cradle To Cradle* model for global developments, currently owns a global design firm and is the dean of architecture at the University of Virginia. He shared his concerns about modern architecture as early as the mid-1970s. "When I was at Yale in 1975, Richard Meier (a world famous contemporary architect) was one of my teachers and he looked at one of my drawings and said, 'young man, solar energy has nothing to do with architecture.' I think Meier took the sole practitioner view and didn't understand how pursuing solar energy as a power source affected a building," says McDonough. "Meier was building structures with giant collapsed walls and lighting facing west and I couldn't live with that. The issue had to do with our culture becoming so timelessly mindless and it was time to become timelessly mindful."[1]

Steven Nielsen, an architect based in Northern California, observed that the 1980 interior and exterior design pastiche shared some things in common with the current explosive changes in the marketing profession. "Besides cars, there's nothing more energy sucking than buildings, and as people who were designing fundamentally ecologically unfriendly things which threaten our sustainability, we (architects) should have been leaders of a green movement.... "Instead, we were pseudo intellectuals trying to please one another, creating our own design problems to solve and doing work which had nothing to do with a social concept or worldly citizenship."[2]

Nielsen's comments are a cautionary tale for marketers. It is tempting to play the role of pseudo-intellectual when it comes to big data, social media, or branding—and lose our grounding in our firms' broader social purpose. The real dialogue must stay centered on improving the customer's condition and the quality of people's lives.

Another design pioneer who was genuinely concerned with the direction of design was Glen Small. Recognized for designing the iconic Biomorphic Biosphere and Green Machine communities between 1965 and 1980, Small introduced concepts for incorporating air purification, collection of water, and vibrant rooftop gardens into residential structures. Small could see the future of our planet, and it wasn't bright. "I read Toffler's predictions of what was coming, a population explosion, and realized the earth couldn't take the impact and the statistics triggered my concerns about food and the environment."[3]

Columnist Luanne Bradley suggests that Small's decades of struggle with the shifting design philosophies "serves as the most compelling evidence that greed superseded social responsibility in the teaching and application of architecture."[4] While many of his contemporaries dubbed Small a misfit, McDonough, Wes Jones, and Bjarke Ingels became acolytes and dedicated their careers to educating organizations on the benefits of marrying sustainable concepts with building beautiful structures.

As a result of these design pioneers—many of whom suffered career setbacks and criticism from cronies—sustainability has become a widely accepted theme today. In fact, Bradley states that "few architects today design without sustainability in mind...LEED Certification and green innovation (have) emerged as the calling cards of the newly informed, earning the respect of the industry and boosting status.[5]

Listen carefully to what McDonough believes about green building standards. He sees them as a process to help architects, builders, and designers create a new standard for excellence. "It's not about certifying what you did yesterday but a celebration of your good intentions for tomorrow," he says.... "Ultimately, it's about materials used again and again with energy from the sun, an endless resourcefulness for our children and what connects all of us together in good will. Design is the first signal of human intention."[6] Setting our intentions plays a key role in mindfulness. If McDonough's theory proves correct, and if human intention is first expressed through design, then how could we incorporate intentionality into our work environments—where our innovation often comes to life?

Designing inspiring, sustainable, and mindful work spaces is a noble concept worth exploring, but it is easier said than done. I spoke with several senior marketers and CEOs about how inspiring they find their work settings and what obstacles they face. They agreed unanimously that technology distractions are the biggest obstacles to creating mindful work environments. These could include the cacophony of multiple workstations and mobile devices beckoning you to respond, or the white noise of office equipment.

Christopher Penn, VP of Marketing Technology for SHIFT Communications, rejects open office plans, ambient noise, and constant digital interruption. "Of all of these, I think digital interruption is by far the worst of all—every device, every app, and every notification is designed to call your attention elsewhere."[7]

Paul Sheng, founder of FoundHere.com, a free website building and hosting company, has learned that "background noise is something we try to avoid...more insidious is the 'always on' mentality that can infect some companies. Regularly incoming email is a major distracter that we haven't gotten a great handle on yet."[8]

After scouring my business community, I discovered a few examples of intentional design. These ten strategies can allay some of these distractions, and several can be deployed with minimal disruption and cost:

1. *Be strategic about team accessibility.* At FoundHere, for example, Sheng says, "We use traditional high wall style cubicles to give everyone their own space. The cubes are clustered into separate areas for each team. By just turning around, they can quietly discuss things. When we need to host meetings, we separate groups off into a room with a closed mostly soundproof door to minimize distractions."[9]

2. *Give it a rest.* An increasing number of companies are making a commitment to help employees reduce stress, enjoy work more often, and think more clearly. Within a short time, I discovered 11 companies that offer meditation rooms and programs. They include
   - Apple,
   - Intel,
   - McKinsey,
   - Prentice Hall Publishing,
   - Google,
   - Nike,
   - AOL Time Warner,
   - Yahoo!,
   - Deutsche Bank,
   - Procter & Gamble, and
   - HBO.[10]

Smaller organizations have also discovered the tangible and intangible benefits of creating silent break rooms. FoundHere.com provides a break room that is located far from the main work areas. Sheng says this helps "create a different context as well as a second quiet break room with a comfortable sleeping couch. I personally find that taking my afternoon break as a short nap can really help me refocus."[11]

3. *Pick a peaceful location.* While every commercial real estate professional knows this innately, it is easy for growing companies to be lured into a sexy new office space that sits beside a bustling freeway or concrete jungle. Instead, Sheng settled on Davis, California, as the location for FoundHere's research and development office "because it's a bike friendly college town. This means lots of parks and greenbelts. Davis has good locally sourced food, tons of restaurants, and a nationally recognized farmers market. Besides being the bike capital of the USA, Davis also has the highest per capita education rate in the country."[12]

4. *Create virtual privacy rituals.* In the SHIFT Communications offices across the United States, Penn says, "we have 'virtual offices,' which are ballistic, over-ear headsets. These are rated −33db noise reduction, and are the same headsets that

you wear when you go to a firing range and shoot rifles. They can transform the most boisterous coworker into a pleasant background noise and eliminate most other noises easily. As a bonus, they're colored bright red and black to indicate that you're working on something important—*don't distract unless you must!*"[13] In open office settings, special headsets send a clear message, and will take the sting out of constant interruptions and unwanted socializing.

5. *Go green and clean.* Can plants make you happier? It's highly possible. *Rodale News'* staff writer Leah Zerbe noted that University of Nevada Cooperative Extension researchers conducted an experiment with 18 elderly assisted-living residents, which involved sponsoring an indoor gardening class. Each participant received a plant to grow at the conclusion of the class. The study found that "interviews at the end of the four-week course showed that the subjects felt more control over their lives and felt healthier and happier than before it started. Five months later, the patients continued to feel that way.... Researchers believe that caring for a houseplant engendered such positive effects because the participants experienced the responsibility of taking care of something other than themselves..."[14] Indoor plants are also proven to be marvelous air purifiers, and can absorb airborne toxins.

6. *Surround yourself with a few inspiring art pieces.* Tatiana Pagés, CEO of Greencard Creative in New York, reminds us of the connection between beauty, creativity, and mindfulness. "Mindfulness is about awareness and empathy. Awareness is about opening yourself up to new perspectives rather than choosing an automatic response... art and design engage the senses and trigger emotions. They are a vehicle to stretch our imagination to see new perspectives and possibilities."

When we see new perspectives, we open the door to greater compassion and empathy—gateways to our *Inner Marketing Guru.* Pagés has found that, in working with global brands such as Diageo and The Allen Morris Company, "design, which is about form and function, creates a lot of empathy because the process forces you to observe and understand human behavior and issues they need solved to make lives better. Art and design evoke empathy, which is an essential part of mindfulness."

She continues, by sharing the consequences of work spaces that are absent of mindful, empathic design. "Many theories exist about the impact of space, color, and forms on people's behavior and emotions. For example, an antiseptic space makes people less empathic. That is why architects and designers are now helping hospitals and psychiatric institutions incorporate more color and shapes into their buildings. It helps evoke a more positive outlook on life…generally, these institutions lack mindfulness."[15]

7. *Let the natural light shine.* It is quite common for professionals—especially home office dwellers—to "place their desk in the darkest corner of the room," says author Laura Vanderkam. "What they've inadvertently done is recreated the corporate cubicle." She recommends that you "move your desk close to the windows, but place it parallel to the panes. This ideal set-up gives you the happiness benefits of natural light, and a good reason to turn away from your computer every few minutes to take in the scene." [16]

8. *Think tasks, not titles.* In some pricey metropolitan areas, such as Tokyo or San Francisco, it is tempting for planners to squeeze as many workers as possible into cubicles. Many companies also create workspaces around employee titles and departments rather than the specific tasks being performed. These industrial-age, penny-pinching strategies are simply counterproductive. Tushar Dave, CEO of start-up Enlighted in Sunnyvale, California, is leading a revolution with lighting and temperature controls that enhance and promote higher employee performance:

> Being mindful in workplace design means taking a systems approach aimed at optimizing team performance based on what they are trying to accomplish.… In the 1970s and 1980s, space designers traditionally focused too much on real estate cost by cramming as many workers as possible into the cheapest spaces and cubicles. Nowadays the most forward thinking companies are looking at space and equipment cost in the context of individual and team needs.

Figure 14.1 Enlighted's Human-Aware Systems detect individual employee activity to create a more comfortable, productive work environment.[17]

Image copyright © Enlighted; used with permission.

Enlighted has introduced a real-time wireless sensor network to create more productive workspaces, and the early results are encouraging. Their systems sense activity and shift lighting "at a granular level, as opposed to binary levels (on/off lighting, warm/cold air controls)." Enlighted's customers report that "as people moved around the office throughout the day, they weren't distracted by environmental factors. On average, these employees increased their productive work hours by an estimated 25 percent."

Individual marketing team contributors have unique needs, and their work spaces must accommodate those needs. Dave and his development teams discovered that "web designers tend to prefer more open spaces and dim lighting to reduce glare on their computer screens. On the other hand, writers tend to prefer more privacy yet brighter light to boost individual based creativity. Investing in more individualized workspaces, rather than expecting all employees to work within similar spaces, vastly boosts employee output."[18]

9. *Be the observer.* By investing a percentage of your time in the "management by walking around" method, you will notice whether your work spaces need a tune-up. Penn at SHIFT has

a mindful and highly effective ritual: "One of the seemingly silliest practices is one I nicknamed after a character from the movie *Office Space*, Bill Lumbergh. It's called *Lumberghing*, in which you walk around the office and casually check in. You can learn a lot about the state of the company just by seeing people's posture, their interactions, etc. Doing so also lets you casually break down silos."[19]

Where will *your* next moment of marketing brilliance happen? Perhaps the office is the last place to look, not the first. Barbara Messing, CMO of TripAdvisor, a travel information hub that attracts over 260 million monthly visitors, says that "for us, mindfulness is the ability to step away from the noise, and give your mind the opportunity to pause, connect and refresh. This practice provides peace of mind so that you can think more deeply and be a strategic marketer."

"We recently had an offsite, and the facilitator asked, "Where are you when you get your best ideas?" Every single team member replied 'outside the office.' That was a big 'aha moment' for us. You're not going to get your best ideas at your desk."[20]

INNER MARKETING GURU Inquiry #14:

What work environment changes will awaken my Inner Marketing Guru?

SECTION 3

The reasonable man adapts himself to the world; the unreasonable one persists in trying to adapt the world to himself. Therefore all progress depends on the unreasonable man.
—George Bernard Shaw

This page intentionally left blank

CHAPTER 15

PEER GROUPS: HOW SHIFTS *REALLY* HAPPEN

Walk with the wise and become wise, for a companion of fools suffers harm.

—Proverbs 13:20

Do you rely mostly on cold-hearted social media sites, Klout scores, and "likes" to guide your career journey, or on a personal force field of trusted peers?

Futurist John Naisbitt, author of *Megatrends* and *High Tech/High Touch: Technology and Our Search for Meaning,* presented and explored this high tech-high touch paradox more than 20 years ago. He predicted that "the more technology we have in this society, the more people want to be with people."[1]

As we are seeing people suffering from "Facebook fatigue" and struggling to find harmony between mindfulness and mindless technology addictions, that concept is coming full circle.

Think about how Naisbitt's prophecy applies to marketing. One-time networking events, faceless awards celebrations, Pinterest pursuits, and customer golf outings are akin to playing a high-octane video game: they feel good when they are happening, but leave little lingering satisfaction when they have ended. In today's overcaffeinated world, marketers need to create strategies to help them design a committed, cohesive offline community of peers and customers who have the potential to transform their careers.

Some may think that LinkedIn, professional association online forums, and other social media outlets create these communities. They simply cannot. They augment human interaction, but they don't replace it. Their main limitation is their inability to express empathy. The value of empathy in our society was a very important finding in psychotherapy in the 1990s. Empathy not only bonds people in social relationships but it also binds people to our brand.

When I spoke with Douglas Van Praet, author of *Unconscious Branding: How Neuroscience Can Empower (and Inspire) Marketing*, we explored the two types of empathy: cognitive and affective empathy—and how they impact relationships:

> With *affective empathy*, you feel others' pain, joy, and sorrow. Neuroscience is teaching us that people don't operate in isolation. Systems and social structures play a very important role in emotions, and our brains are often designed to synchronize with other humans. Empathy is triggered by direct stimulation, not rationality and reasoning. When we see someone fall down, for example, we feel their pain at some level. When you feel people's emotions, you are much more willing to help them."[2]

The second type, *cognitive empathy*, is expressed when someone says, "I understand how you are feeling, but I don't feel it myself." Cognitive empathy is the bedrock of most marketing research initiatives. Think of all the times marketers have been the detached observers of a live focus group or pored over reports for common themes and "buyer personas," a trendy term that business to business (B2B) companies use to identify their ideal customer.

Van Praet believes "we are hard wired for both types of empathy, yet we have two competing drives within us. Business leaders generally choose the cognitive route. This makes us more inclined towards aggressive, competitive behavior—which is from our evolutionary days where we needed to survive and dominate others."[3] One discipline that falls squarely in the cognitive empathy camp is the use of predictive analytics and big data. In my experience, heavy dependency on big data at the expense of mindfulness and empathic behaviors creates a one-dimensional brand.

When people lack any empathy, they exhibit psychopathic behavior. Van Praet has learned that "when an executive says 'it's not about peace and love, it's about business models and the bottom line,'" there is a good chance they have trouble retaining great people and developing lifelong customer relationships.[4] Personally, I have seen my share of psychopathic, self-centered behavior in the sales and marketing ranks.

Figure 15.1 Customer Advisory Board

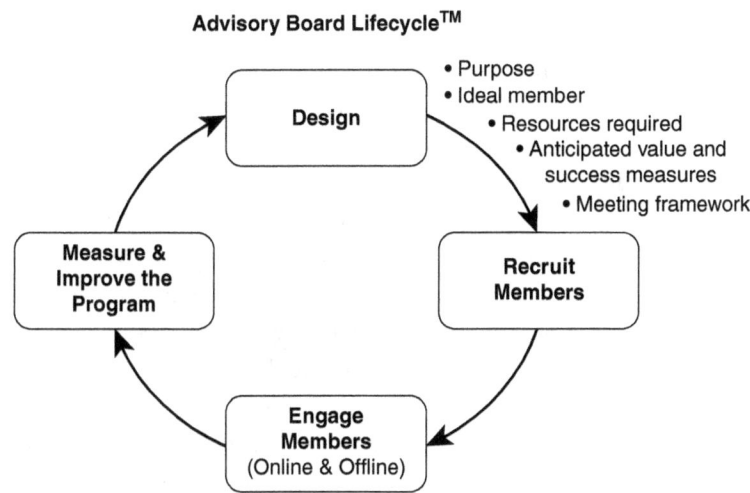

Copyright 2014, Lisa Nirell. All rights reserved.

This is why the development of supportive communities will grow in importance for people to realize professional and personal success. These groups allow us to sit across the table from peers and nurture affective empathy. Van Praet is helping CEOs and marketing leaders design these human qualities into their go-to market and branding initiatives.

Two types of communities can help mindful marketers foster these qualities: peer groups and formal Customer Advisory Boards (CABs). We will investigate the benefits of both, and ways to optimize your participation in these sacred, influential circles.

A *peer group* enables a group of 8–12 contemporaries to grow and learn together in a private, confidential setting. A CAB is usually designed to accomplish two key things: to convene a small group of 6–10 customers so that a company can gain unfiltered feedback on their strategic goals and offerings, and to allow customers to grow together. Neither should be confused with annual conferences, recognition events, user groups, networking groups, or social gatherings.

Peer groups and CABs have two things in common: they are designed as private learning communities, and they follow a common four-step process to sustain and grow (see Figure 15–1).

1. *Design (defining the purpose, ideal member, resources required, anticipated value and success measures, and meeting framework)*
2. *Recruit Members*

3. *Engage Members (online and offline)*
4. *Measure and Improve the program*

Bruce Peters, franchisee of Renaissance Executive Forums of upstate New York, has actively managed several CEO peer groups. He has witnessed an evolution in how peer groups operate, and the relentless demand on the group facilitator to continually grow and filter information for members. "The biggest change in the past 13 years has been the shift in the volume of information. Today, the facilitator must spend more time as a knowledge aggregator than ever before. When I started in 2000, there were not as many peer group options and alternatives. Associations, franchises, and other organizations have recently created their own variations. This makes it tougher for peer group leaders to differentiate themselves."[5]

In spite of the increased competition for members, Peters believes that peer groups will thrive in the years to come. The group leader is often the key differentiator, and provides value far beyond their facilitation skills. "Today's leader must have a deep *and* broad set of experiences to understand the issues at hand. They need to be committed to lifelong learning, exhibit deep listening skills, ask probing questions, be perpetually curious, and understand each member's goals."[6]

Mindful, high-performing peer groups have several qualities in common:

1. *Members get naked (figuratively) in front of one another.* It is easy for a member to bring a tactical question to the group that actually is a symptom of a deeper issue. Peters adds, "My members bring their real issues to the group. They are willing to be vulnerable. I ask new potential members, 'Do you believe that you get out of the group what you put into it?' to assess their fit in the group.[7]
2. *The members protect confidentiality at all costs.* In my CMO groups, I call this the Vegas rule: What happens in the room stays in the room. The sacred space cannot thrive without this understanding.
3. *They create rituals.* Alison Whitmire, principal at C-lever Biz, has built and sustained several high-performing CEO peer groups in her career. "We start and end our meetings with a moment of silence, the intent of which is to create the container, or to bracket the sacred space we are creating. I believe

that peer groups have the power to accelerate an individual's coming into full self-expression, and that becomes the official or unofficial agenda of the work. The more mindfully that the work can be done, the more complete the journey to full expression can be."[8]

4. *They set clean intentions.* I have integrated Cathy and Gary Hawk's Check-In Process™[9] into every live CMO meeting to help us reinforce this behavior. Each person spends two to three minutes sharing "What's different? What worked in my performance this month? What didn't work? For what am I grateful?" And finally, "What are my intentions today?"

   Whitmire affirms that in high-performing groups, "members are challenged to be the best version of themselves in ways that are caring and with clean intention. A clean intention is one that is for the sole purpose of bettering the other person. An unclean intention can be challenging someone because I think they are wrong and I want to be right, I want to look good, or I have some ego-based reason for the challenge."[10]

5. *They establish norms.* Every peer group should share a common set of values and nonnegotiable ways of operating. In my peer groups, the norms are outlined in the Member Agreement, which members sign. In order to maintain active membership status, they must agree to these norms:
   - They must respond promptly to requests from the group.
   - They must attend a minimum number of live meetings each year.
   - They must maintain confidentiality at all times.
   - They must be willing to be generous with the other members.

Whitmire takes these norms one step further. "We have NO tolerance for members judging other members. People are judging other people all the time, comparing them with how they 'should' be, labeling them with minimal information about them, or believing that they are 'less than' for some reason. It happens to some degree in every group, whether it is voiced or not. Judgment separates. Acceptance binds."[11]

6. *They ask and don't tell.* Peters emphasizes that "the best groups don't give you an answer; they help you build a process that

helps YOU discover your answer. Accountability becomes a byproduct of this practice. High-performing teams just naturally hold each other accountable. In executive-level peer groups, we are modeling that behavior so that they bring that accountability process back to their companies." [12]

Many of these same practices can shape successful CABs as well. Unfortunately, many companies become internally focused and forget to deliver value to their own customers. This is a natural temptation during times of leadership transition and major market shifts.

Recently the managing partner of a professional service firm was inspired to launch a CAB, and needed between 8–12 committed customers to launch the group. Her intention was to create a sounding board where she could share insights on her firm's growth plans, gather candid feedback to inform the plan, and foster deeper client relationships. As she designed her list of ideal invitees, she experienced an epiphany. She decided to invite her biggest customer—a well-known billionaire—to join as a CAB charter member. This would appeal to the other candidates and help her fill the board seats within weeks versus months.

She was convinced that this billionaire would enhance their brand repute and customer-retention rate. In reality, it was apparent that the billionaire was too distracted to make any long-term commitment. If she had followed through with her plan, and had he agreed, he would have missed most of the meetings. His absence would have created group dissension, and she would have been forced to eventually remove him from the board. This could have easily damaged their relationship and future revenue potential.

Thankfully, she averted this risky move. Instead, she created a special recognition event exclusively for this customer. Had she not taken a step back to carefully design the CAB, she may have been facing some dicey customer conversations.

PURPOSE OF A CAB

A Customer Advisory Board CAB helps firms accelerate innovation, deepen customer relationships, and provide value-added, confidential discussion forums for customers and industry allies. While researching 30 companies that have deployed successful CABs, I found that they had several common traits:

- They are sincerely growth oriented.
- They believe in gathering unfiltered feedback to refine their future plans and services.
- They are passionate about developing trusted adviser-level relationships and making a difference in their industry.
- They swiftly adapt the group to industry and regulatory shifts to ensure continuity.
- They are willing to implement CAB recommendations

CAB PLANNING IS KEY

Companies often underestimate the time and energy required to design and build a sustainable CAB. Recruiting ideal members can take as long as nine months. (Coincidentally, the same holds true for peer group design and recruitment). Here are nine steps to designing a powerful CAB:

1. *Define the CAB's purpose.* When I spoke with Simon Angove, CEO of GMT Corporation, he outlined his four key CAB goals:
   - *Engage their customers in early-release programs* so they can act as references when the product is released.
   - *Allow customers to formally influence their products' strategic direction.* He has found that this step results in a better-quality product that closely matches customer requirements and is field proven.
   - *Treat the board members as "trusted advisers"* to GMT to help them evaluate trends, and guide them on how GMT can act on those trends.
   - *Provide a formal channel* through which customers can share best practices and offer advice.

   GMT has boasted a 95 percent customer retention rate over the past five years, and says the CAB played a key role in driving this success.[13]

2. *Create a clear profile of the ideal CAB member.* Before you invite any customers, document the characteristics of an ideal member. For example, do you want them to be influential industry pundits? Are they passionate about some aspect of your business, such as employee development and retention, marketing, or federal tax laws? If you strictly invite your biggest customers or industry celebrities, you may later be thrust

into the uncomfortable position of having to fire that over-committed member.

3. *Give yourself ample time to recruit members.* Bob Arciniaga, founder of Advisory Board Architects, has helped dozens of companies build their CABs. He says it typically takes 150 hours and four to six months to identify and recruit members. Provide member candidates ample time to consider your invitation; with their busy schedules, they may need at least a month.[14]

4. *Establish clear expectations with potential new members.* It's common practice to request customers to commit at least five days per year to prepare, convene, and debrief.

5. *Keep the group small and intimate.* Among the companies I interviewed, those with longstanding, highly collaborative groups averaged six to fifteen members. When groups grow larger, they are forced to divide the group into special interest areas, and managing discussions can become unwieldy.

6. *Mix it up.* Colin Gounden, CEO of Via Science, hosts a board that comprises an equal numbers of existing customers, top-tier customers, and a few prospects. The group also includes one or two industry experts. He has found that a variety of backgrounds creates a magnetic effect.[15]

7. *Address the compensation issue early.* At a minimum, plan on covering out-of-town members' travel and living expenses. If participants are located near your main office, host a modest but memorable event at an upscale location. As a special bonus, consider donating fees to their favorite charity. Some firms deduct their advisory board fee (typically $500–$1,000) from a future invoice.

8. *Develop a written advisory board member agreement.* This should include an indemnification clause that holds members harmless from any damages, losses, suits, and fines against your firm. The agreement should also stipulate time expectations and grounds for termination.

9. *Stay fluid.* Keep one or two new member candidates in mind for the future. Since every CAB has a shelf life, be prepared to replace some members every year. As your company reaches the next level of growth and celebrates certain milestones, you will need a different talent mix.

HOW TO KEEP CABS RUNNING SMOOTHLY

Let's say you have succeeded in the first two important steps in your CAB strategy: design and recruitment. Now you need the essentials for completing a successful first year. It begins with a solid meeting framework, strong customer engagement systems, and a reliable follow-up strategy. Much like peer group models, the ability to lead effective customer conversations in a safe, confidential setting is equally important.

1. *Allocate ample meeting preparation time.* Well-established CAB leaders indicated that it is not unusual for each executive sponsor to invest at least 15–20 hours per quarter in preparatory activity. Provide the agenda at least a week in advance to participants, and don't be shy about requesting they complete homework in advance.
2. *Select locations conducive to creative thinking and collaboration.* Choose modestly upscale retreat settings over overstimulating adult playgrounds. The managing partner of a $3M management consulting firm based in Seattle chose Las Vegas for an upcoming advisory board meeting, and regretted his choice of location.
3. *Create a collaborative container at every meeting.* Effective customer board meetings begin with a clear purpose and ground rules. Marnie Ochs-Raleigh, CEO of Evolve Systems, says, "During the CAB, you should not complain about other customers, employees, or competitors. Instead, focus on what is going well and what needs to improve. While introducing each person to the group, I also explain why they were chosen to participate, and provide a 30-second commercial about their skill set and business."[16]
4. *Balance structure with white space.* Ask for topics ahead of time, assign homework, and then schedule dedicated time on the agenda for open discussion. This increases the value of the meetings. Customers begin using each other as support groups when they are not in session, and new topics naturally emerge for future gatherings.
5. *Engage seasoned external CAB experts.* A facilitator is seen as a neutral party. According to Luc Vezina, CEO of Vanilla Forums, "it really helps to have an outside facilitator. We feel uncomfortable

telling a very loud customer to allow time for other members to contribute."[17] This encourages open participation and allows members to feel less pressure from the company concerning their responses. Companies such as The Geehan Group and Advisory Board Architects can minimize costly trial and error.

6. *Create forums for regular interaction.* Ian Knox, VP of Worldwide Marketing for Daptiv, a privately held technology company based in Seattle, Washington, suggests smaller lunch breakout groups and discussion topics. Daptiv also invites well-known industry analysts as guest speakers.[18] Some B2B organizations have customers who are very comfortable using web-based collaboration tools.

7. *Implement the best ideas.* You want the CAB members to feel heard and valued, so be sure to respond quickly to their recommendations and implement the best ones. Every CAB host should share meeting minutes immediately following the gatherings.

8. *Conduct meaningful return-on-investment (ROI) analysis.* One technology company tracks the rate of customer advocate growth and innovation that is spawned by the group. As a result of implementing some of the recommended CAB innovations, one company exceeded their product sales goal by 20 percent.

In another instance, a global irrigation company tracks both the number of individual product improvement submissions received and attainment of year-to-date product sales goals. Their VP of Marketing told me that they would have probably met these goals without the Council, but it would have taken significantly more time, and their research and development costs would have been higher. You can also consider tracking customer retention and renewals.

You face a universe of possible ways to engage peers and customers. When choosing between cold-hearted computer interaction and the Force, choose the latter. When the Force is with you, every participant will savor the opportunity to be heard.

INNER MARKETING GURU Inquiry #15:

What are my intentions for creating or joining a peer group?

CHAPTER 16

WHAT THE CEO WANTS THE CMO TO KNOW

Irrigators channel waters, fletchers straighten arrows, carpenters bend wood, the wise master themselves.

—Buddha[1]

Modern marketers can deftly recite the ABCs of content marketing, revenue performance management, social media, and branding to their peers. Yet when it comes to conversations with the CEO, marketing leaders often speak Greek.

One of my clients committed such a major communications faux pas that he was forced to resign. Barry, an accomplished PhD with a background in life sciences, worked for a $75M organization, and reported directly to the CEO. His official title was VP of Sales and Marketing. One of his top annual objectives was to create a new website for his organization. The site would ostensibly enhance an existing web platform, which was fully operable but limited in functionality. The new site was intended to drive at least 30 percent of product revenues by December 2014. The purpose of the merchant site was twofold: the organization wanted to provide customers with multiple and flexible ordering options, and the company wanted to reach new markets.

Barry hired the best web team available. Together, they developed a project plan with clear milestones and accountabilities. The team committed to a specific launch date for the online store. The VP promised the CEO that the new store would be meet their revenue and 100 percent online availability targets, and that his deployment team was highly capable. On paper, the plan was attainable. They were simply enhancing an existing site, and initially added just a few products to the site to ensure the service worked properly. Over time, his team would add a more robust merchant account capability. What could possibly go wrong?

On the day of the new site launch, several things went terribly wrong. The VP discovered that the web team forgot to conduct a series of critical tests before flipping the production switch. Barry, a naturally optimistic leader, had never set realistic expectations with the CEO prior to the launch date, nor did he provide frequent updates. That seemed unnecessary at the time, since he did not anticipate any potential setbacks or outages.

In the end, the relaunch of the site was a dismal disappointment. Several days passed before customers could order products online. The company lost tens of thousands of dollars in sales during those few days. The VP's daily status meetings with the CEO, CFO, and customer service became boiler room bickering sessions and a lesson in micro-management. Barry had lost the trust and respect of the CEO, which had taken him several years to earn. Within 30 days, the CEO stripped Barry of all sales responsibilities and soon hired a VP of Sales—without involving Barry in the hiring process.

This is a harsh reminder of the importance of overcommunicating with your leadership team, and setting realistic, yet aggressive, expectations with your CEO. I'm a "glass half-full" person, but that doesn't give me—nor any of my peers—an excuse to ignore potential risk.

As you assess your current relationship with your CEO, how would you rate yourself on a scale of 1–10? Do you feel like a fish out of water at level 1 *("Those guys just don't understand Marketing!")*? Or, are you and the CEO rowing in the same direction at level 10 *("We are crystal clear on our top 3–4 objectives and program risks, and discuss progress on a regular basis")*?

If you gave yourself a low score between 1 and 5, you are not alone. Persuasion and effective communication are often taken for granted. I know I have made some false assumptions in the past. In fact, I assumed that marketing leaders were dynamos of discourse and experts of enticement. The data tell us something very different:

- In early 2013, I surveyed and interviewed 45 senior marketing leaders. The top two challenges they reportedly experienced in their current roles included "lack of self-leadership" and "poor access to resources and funding." The common self-leadership deficiencies they shared included an inability to manage their time, lack of insight into the future, constant firefighting and poor life balance.

> A dearth of self-leadership skills lowers self-confidence, as well as the vitality that is required to thrive in this volatile profession. Several leaders have shared that concern privately with me. Low self-confidence leads to poor persuasive abilities, which makes communication less effective. Ineffective communication prevents leaders from creating a sense of urgency among peers, and a lack of urgency reduces the potential to prioritize. If you cannot influence your company's priorities, you become irrelevant.

- In his latest best-selling book, *To Sell is Human*, Daniel Pink shares the results of his survey of 7,000 executives. The survey revealed that 41–70 percent of their time is spent selling *something*, which can include ideas, products, services, bigger budget requests, and new initiatives. The activity of selling can be cash-driven selling (such as a real estate broker), or it can be selling ideas (such as a senior executive jockeying for more resources). Yet few marketers are formally educated in the art of selling and persuasion.[2] And, within my own CMO community, less than one-tenth of the marketers have ever carried a sales quota.
- CEOs are funding more marketing programs to increase access to "sales intelligence" and drive more organic sales growth, but they are not seeing those investments translate into higher revenues. In fact, the CSO Insights 2013 Sales Performance Optimization Study revealed that sales intelligence usage rose from 62 percent to 67 percent over the time period they tracked. In addition, over 40 percent of the twelve hundred sales executives surveyed reported that they need help prioritizing and researching new accounts, and less than two-thirds of the professionals indicated they are making quota. If marketing leaders are providing large quantities and sources of data, why are their efforts not generating the anticipated returns?[3]

When we ignore the need to continually refine our persuasion abilities, we bypass the opportunity to evolve into the *Super CMO* role. In my client community, I have discovered three qualities that define Super CMOs and are essential to working with the CEO. These are outlined in Figure 16–1. These qualities include

1. *Customer Focus*—this reflects a solid understanding of buyer behavior, positioning, marketing automation, customer relationship management (CRM), the buyer's experience (or journey), and analytics to align campaigns with buyer behaviors. It also represents the marketing team's ability to understand the company's customer philosophy and translate that into a cogent message across every communications avenue.
2. *Persuasion*—the ability to communicate effectively with customers, Board, and teams using appropriate analytical and reporting tools to help you get what you want and appease their self-interest.
3. *Agility*—the ability to adapt to new competitors, changes in customer behaviors and priorities, nascent technology trends, shifts in strategy, employee attrition, Board-level expectations, and personal setbacks.

Absence of mastery in any of these areas leads to (1) *irrelevance*, (2) *ineffectiveness*, or (3) *inflexibility*.

I have been searching for the causes of CMO skill deficiencies and conflicts with the CEO. I found five potential culprits.

Figure 16.1   The Super CMO Zone

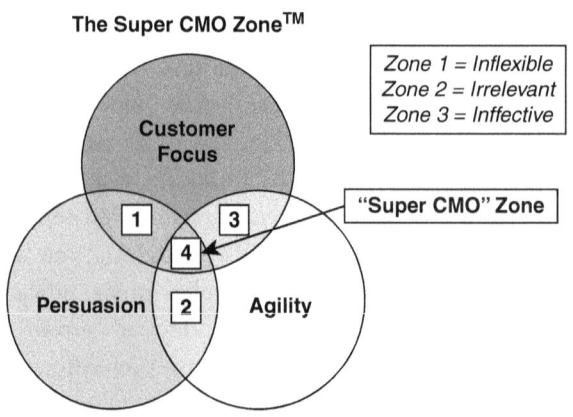

Copyright 2014, Lisa Nirell. All rights reserved.

First, CMOs often speak a different language from CEOs. In my experience, marketing leaders often *revel* in their use of unique language. As we discussed in chapter 2, the "CEOs are from Mars; Marketing is from Venus" aphorism is alive and well. The CFO and the VP of Sales typically use the same format to report earnings and revenues. They refer to *pipeline, revenue, backlog,* and *return on investment.* Marketing, on the other hand, loves to discuss *Twitter followers, lead scoring, social media, publicity buzz, and events.* In the CEO's mind, marketing creates divisiveness and distractions from their number one priority: reporting predictable results to investors and shareholders. Often the CMO leaves it up to the CEO to make the connection between *publicity buzz* and *revenues.* This is an unfair and presumptuous move on the part of the CMO.

Second, CMOs have historically reported intangible benefits and outcomes, which run counter to how CEOs are measured and evaluated by investors and boards. In the past, it was virtually impossible to attribute sales to specific marketing activities, such as content delivery, events, or demand creation. I am a big believer that brand and culture stewardship rest squarely on the CMO's shoulders, and they are essential to the future success of any organization. That does not mean, however, that the CMO is immune to the growing demand of demonstrating value of their efforts.

Third, most CMOs are not well educated in the area of marketing analytics tools—yet the CEO expects them to report quantitative results. Analytics have forever changed the CEO's expectations on marketing. As of this writing, a small percentage of marketing leaders have hired data scientists to help them decode the big data puzzle. In order to thrive in today's economy, marketing's hunches and intuition must be accompanied by some supporting data. For example, both the CEO and the board expect the CMO to benchmark their performance against competitors and industry peers, and then test their assumptions. Without it, marketers could be paying excessive sums for marketing research, talent, web designers, social media experts, and standard agency services.

The best way to lose your CEO's confidence is to pepper the conversation with a litany of tactical activities, such as trade shows, awards, sponsorships, and Twitter campaigns. By contrast, successful CMOs frame executive level meeting discussions by reportingtheir progress against activities that are driving revenue and brand equity. Furthermore, they can show how they are tracking against industry or previous benchmark data.

Fourth, Marketing often does not align with the reporting cadence of the rest of the organization. Most companies embrace a certain weekly, monthly, quarterly, and annual reporting rhythm. While the VP of Sales reports how your company is tracking against forecast, the CFO reports on how earnings, revenues, and renewals compare to previous quarters. The VP of Customer Support shares progress with the Net Promoter Score. Conversely, the VP of Marketing typically reverts to a "Greek" reporting cadence. They may report on the latest social media campaign, a customer briefing, or a big trade show at one meeting. Then, in subsequent months, they report on a completely different set of activities. How can the CEO keep track of these disparate activities? If that behavior describes you, then you are inadvertently alienating yourself and your department from the rest of the organization.

Finally, Marketing leaders fear, versus embrace, the numbers. One of my clients is the CEO of a high-growth company. Privately, he shared that "what's hard is that the Marketing VP does not want to lead their portion of the meeting with metrics." During his tenure with one company, he hired three different CMOs—and every one resisted his request to provide the same presentation outline for prescheduled status meetings. Something as straightforward as saying, "Here is what we are tracking; here's where we are; here's where we are going, and here is what we are working on this week" was a foreign concept—or at least one that they resisted. This aversion to including metrics causes even greater dissonance between Marketing and the rest of the senior executive team members.

These five causes of CEO misalignment are not insurmountable. I recommend these strategies to help you thrive and secure a seat in the power circle

1. *Break down your CEO influencing strategy into steps.* The purpose of communicating a compelling message in the CEO's language is to generate interest. Interest generates a meeting; meetings build trusting relationships, and relationships drive mutual agreement. A mutual agreement contains business goals, measures of success, and the overall value to the organization, customers, employees, shareholders, and community. When you have forged a mutual agreement, you can build a business case that reaches the "high priority" list. Ultimately, this sequence of events builds trust with the CEO.

2. *Align your executive meeting reports, reporting cadence, and language with your department peers (including finance and sales).* Report on your annual and quarterly progress against key metrics first. Ensure you report on demand creation activities in the early portion of meetings. Downplay highlights on tactical issues, such as a logo design, Twitter campaigns, website updates, or customer events. They can be reported on a "need-to-know" basis or in an email summary. When you prepare for a board meeting, be sure your slides are designed to look and sound consistent with the others being presented.
3. *Select marketing key performance indicators (KPIs) that align with your portfolio of products and services.* Some products and services require as many as 5–7 years before they contribute scalable revenues and profits to an organization. Over time, companies attempt to implement systems and processes to move those products across a time horizon to ensure they eventually generate a healthy, predictable stream of revenues. Some succeed; others cling to the past and watch products wither and die before they reach market maturity.

As a marketer, you must set expectations with your CEO that you will be investing different levels of your marketing budget to products based on their projected revenue contribution timeline. Marketers must promote their portfolio of products and services differently as they reach different points on the time horizon. During the early market acceptance stage, for example, it is common to invest heavily in publicity, thought leadership content, and selling activities that drive early adoption.

Figure 16.2, based on the Three Horizons Model developed by McKinsey & Company,[4] provides guidance on which performance metrics matter in their evolution. Some rest squarely in the current time horizon, or Horizon 1, and have reached a certain level of scale. The organization can deliver them efficiently and predictably. Horizon 2 products and services are on the path to scaling, and do not yet deliver steady profits. In fact, some Horizon 2 products remain in "no man's land," and the company never delivers financial and performance systems that allow the products to scale.

Horizon 3 products and services live squarely in "new market category" territory. They require you to track a different set of metrics than

Figure 16.2 The Three Time Horizons Model

Managing a Portfolio: The Three Horizons Model

Time Frame	Horizon 1 (0–12 months)	Horizon 2 (12–36 months)	Horizon 3 (36–72 months)
Driving Goal	Maximize Economic Returns	Become a going concern	Create a new category
Key Performance Indicators	• Revenue vs. plan • Bookings • Contribution margin • Market share • Wallet share	• Target accounts vs. plan • Sales velocity • Average deal size • Segment share • Time to tipping point	• Name brand customers • Deal size • Name brand partners • PR and social media buzz • Flagship products

Low ———————————————→ High
Resources Needed to Generate Revenue

Source: McKinsey & Company, used with permission.

products that fall within Horizon 3, because they are not expected to generate revenues for up to 72 months. In fact, you may find yourself jockeying for attention and resources from the profitable, successful Horizon 3 teams, and can expect some stiff resistance. At times, your Horizon 3 marketing efforts may even be ignored.

Work beside your CEO to reevaluate your KPIs as products mature, migrate closer toward Horizon 1, and become more widely accepted by the marketplace.

4. *Ask the CEO and the CFO what they want to see on the reports.* Create a custom report that reflects the company's top 3–4 priorities, as well as your progress against your department's top three performance goals. Set your ego aside and put the CEO's KPIs at the top of the report. While yours may seem most important, strategic KPI placement will earn some respect from the CEO.

If you are relatively new to your role, find a way to quickly prove that you understand your company's target market and share your insights across the organization. This will help you demonstrate your expertise and value quickly. Joe Dunsmore, CEO and chairman of Digi International, offers this advice: "I want the CMO to focus on strategic marketing and to explain our target market. This needs to be based on a nuanced understanding of our customer—they should look at wins and losses for behavioral and buying patterns, and be able to define the ideal customer in great detail. Their insights help our research and development, sales, and product management teams invest their resources wisely."[5]

5. *Stay agile.* Sometimes reporting on the numbers needs to take a back seat to dramatic market shifts, new competitors, time-sensitive "first mover" opportunities, and team attrition. They may need to be included in an upcoming executive meeting agenda. If you are working with nascent products and services in time Horizon 3, for example, then share progress on the number of high-profile, name-brand partners and accounts you have secured. At this stage, early market wins are more important metrics than revenue attainment against plan.

6. *Tell the bad news first.* Transparency drives trust. Joe Payne reminds us that "If *I* know that *you* know, then I can trust you will solve the problem. Tell me the bad news immediately, and show me a way you are going to fix it. If you don't talk about your plan and your progress, then you are in a bad place. And I will assume you don't even *know* you are in a bad place. That's when I need to find someone else to fill your shoes."[6]

These communication and reporting strategies will earn you a seat at the table. Once the CEO recognizes that you care about revenues, and can report on the results of your marketing investments, you will evolve into a new role: the trusted marketing adviser. That title translates into "success" in every language.

INNER MARKETING GURU Inquiry #16:

What daily practices will help me improve my credibility and financial acumen with the CEO?

This page intentionally left blank

CHAPTER 17

CFO-SPEAK: MINDFUL MARKETING BY THE NUMBERS

Waste neither time nor money, but make the best use of both.
—Benjamin Franklin

I t was 1984, and the personal computer revolution was well underway. I was working for one of the world's first commercially successful PC software companies, MultiMate International. We disrupted the word-processing industry by displacing stand-alone devices from now-defunct companies such as Digital Equipment (DEC) and Wang. Will Jones, the CEO, was a fun-loving software genius at heart, and often roller-skated down the corridors of our converted warehouse offices to boost morale.

We doubled in size for several consecutive years and watched revenues soar. As the International Marketing Manager, I did my best to keep up the pace. In those heady days, the priority was closing business and selling as many licenses to my distributors as I could, not managing profit margins. I seldom communicated with the finance team—that was the VP of Sales and Marketing's job. Instead, I spoke the language of publicity, marketing programs, events management, and managing channel partners.

During one summer afternoon in 1985, the business temporarily came to a halt when Jones sold MultiMate to Ashton-Tate, and immediately laid off half of the company. While he shared the bad news with each employee, including me, he wore his roller skates, jeans, and a terribly loud and annoying bright yellow t-shirt. It bore a smiley face and the caption "Happiness is Positive Cash Flow."

I quickly realized, at the ripe age of 23, that growth at any price had a cost, and consolidation was a necessary, yet ugly, part of the cycle of industry maturity.

I am probably not the only marketing person who has felt clueless in the face of a liquidity event. In my experience, finance fundamentals are often passed on through the school of trial and error, not through formal education. We slowly learn the basics, such as the most critical roles that a CFO must fulfill. These include controllership, financial planning and analysis (FP&A), information technology (IT) and human resources (HR) management, treasury (forecast cash and liquidity relative to short-term and long-term working capital; Accounts Payable management), and strategy (valuation drivers, relations with external advisers, investment bankers, attorneys, etc.). Sadly, that's not enough for a mindful marketer to thrive, because the CFO role is changing.

Two pivotal shifts are affecting CFOs today, and will impact marketers in untold ways:

- *Trend #1: Finance has greater influence and authority over operations and IT.* According to Gary Patterson, CEO of advisory firm Fiscal Doctor, Inc., "in companies ranging from 50M–$1B, today's CFOs are expected to play the role of both COO [chief operating officer] and CFO, which is even more of a strategic position."[1] This means that your CFO may also be responsible for additional activities such as prioritizing a finite set of company resources, communicating the strategy across the company, implementing performance and recognition programs, and overseeing staffing levels and team incentives to fulfill the company's requirements.

The CFO is also increasingly involved in overseeing strategic technology investments. *CFO Innovation Asia* reported in December 2013 that in some countries, organizations are also seeing finance gaining more control over IT decisions: "nearly 83% of respondents [in the Robert Half study are] citing a rise in collaboration between the IT and finance teams during the last three years—a sign that IT will be integrated into financial performance planning, and the lines between the IT department and finance will continue to blur as technology becomes the valued enabler, rather than the end game."[2]

Don Clarke, a seasoned CFO based in Washington DC, suggests that this is a trend whose time has come. He has advised CEOs for over two decades, and overseen multiple liquidity events and public offerings. In today's economy, he finds that "the CFO role is morphing towards a key business partner to the CEO. They both share something in common, and are unique in that they have to worry about the whole 'family': developers, HR, IT, Sales, and Marketing."[3]

What are the implications for CMOs? The CFO will expect marketers to speak the language of numbers and strategy more than ever before. It will be harder to justify your marketing budget unless you are capable of explaining how those marketing investments will benefit other departments and your customers.

- *Trend #2: Marketing and sales incentive plans and IT investments will require different reporting standards.* The International Financial Reporting Standards (IFRS) are gradually being deployed to help public companies implement one set of global accounting standards. The intent is to facilitate growth and make it easier for investors and global teams to review and understand financial statements. The Financial Accounting Standards Board (FASB) is the governing body. So far, public companies in the European Union (EU), Israel, New Zealand, Mexico, Canada, and Brazil have embraced the new standard. Once these standards are fully deployed in the United States, which is projected to happen in 2015, the accounting profession will face fundamental shifts.

    CMOs have two options in this new IFRS scenario: to proactively work with their finance counterparts on a plan to adopt these new reporting standards into the marketing planning and budgeting cycles, or to watch what happens and respond hastily. The consequence of option two is further dissonance with finance.

It may take time for these trends to take hold in your organization. Until then, you can avoid these common measurement mistakes, which further alienate you from your finance team:

1. *Jumping to hasty conclusions.* Let's say that you launch a new website, and you generate a marketing campaign to promote the new features and offers. Soon after launch, website traffic

spikes significantly. Your analytics reports tell you that visitors are spending a significantly longer time on the pages you feature. According to Larry Freed, former CEO of ForeSee and author of *Innovating Analytics*, many of us would immediately conclude that our launch was a big success: "Is that page great, or is it problematic? Visitors may love the content, or they may be getting stuck because of a problem on the page."[4]

2. *Relying too heavily on historical information.* Freed continues by saying, "Many analytics programs are dominated by behavioral data. Behavioral data tell us what has happened, not what *will* happen. We may have visited, purchased, downloaded, registered, or whatever else the company is looking for us to do. Will we do it again? That depends on if our needs were met and we had a high level of satisfaction with the experience."[5]

3. *Confusing feedback with measurement.* Freed defines measurement as "a random sample of consumers that gives us data that are representative of the broader audience. Feedback is unsolicited by the company and either is direct from the consumer to the company, or indirect from the consumer via social networks.[6] Since the feedback generated on social networks is very difficult to track, if not impossible, the most vocal naysayers may never be counted. (I discussed the dangers of "Dark Social" in another chapter.) Furthermore, your biggest fans may seldom provide you with unsolicited feedback. It is crucial to avoid the temptation to make wholesale changes to your marketing plan or product strategy as a result of limited customer feedback.

4. *Gaming the system.* The most common method that marketers use for gaming the system is to offer customers incentives to participate in your market research, and motivating employees to deploy strong-arm techniques to extract perfect satisfaction scores from their customers. I personally experienced the latter when I owned a Mercedes convertible. Within seconds of signing my service paperwork at the dealership, the service adviser said, "Our customer service team will be calling you to ensure you received 5-star service today. My team is given bonuses based on your scores. May I count on you to give us a perfect score?" I found this to be manipulative and perfunctory.

Freed advises us to "avoid incenting people to complete surveys, especially when there is no need. Never ask for personal data; some customers will decline to participate for privacy or confidentiality concerns. And try to prevent your staff from asking or begging their customers to give them good scores."[7]

What steps can a CMO do to earn more credibility with their CFO and fuel more innovations? In three words, financial language fluency. Here are more detailed recommendations:

1. Bolster your competence around marketing planning and forecasting. This requires you to be transparent with the CFO. Here's how. First, identify marketing on metrics that matter. Pick ones that align with your overall corporate objectives and the stage of growth your company is experiencing—not metrics that you think are "cool."

    I have often seen CMOs in start-ups track industry influencer coverage and new account revenues. Conversely, an established mid-market company may opt to track customer retention rates, pipeline velocity, customer wallet share, or brand repute. Your CFO usually reports on a broader set of metrics such as free cash flow, operating margins, revenue growth, and shareholder value.

    Want to dazzle the CFO? Show them your anticipated spending plan for the next 90 days. This helps the CFO project cash flow, which is a particularly important topic for start-ups and fast-growth companies. Also, keep your progress reports consistent from one fiscal period to the next. This demonstrates that you have a good sense of what is happening in your organization.

2. Reinforce the term *value creation*, not *marketing expense*. While some activities in your integrated marketing plan will focus on short-term wins, brand development can often take five years to manage and measure. Educate your CFO on the importance of tracking both leading (behavioral) and trailing indicators (results) across the customer relationship spectrum. As a mindful marketer, you are a market maker, not an order taker.

    In Figure 17.1, Freed offers a holistic model to capture a complete picture of your customers and the experience they

Figure 17.1   The Customer Experience Measurement Ecosystem Graphic

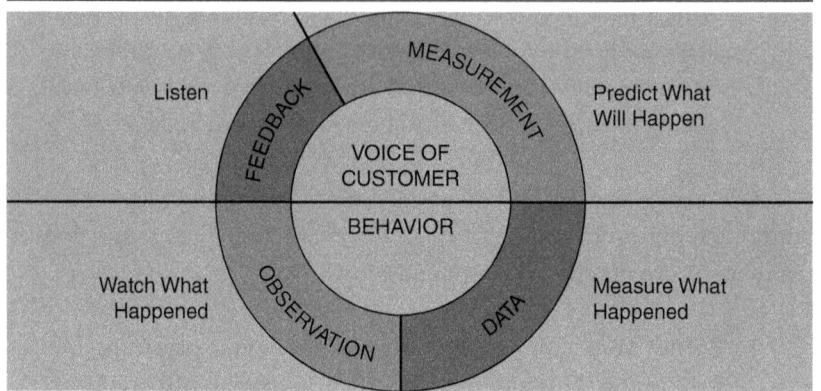

Courtesy of Larry Freed.

are having at each point. The fundamental elements of the Customer Experience Ecosystem include *behavioral data, feedback or service data, observation,* and *the customer experience.*[8]

3. Agree with the CFO on what categories will be created for allocating funds. In a typical marketing plan, categories might include
   - global campaigns,
   - customer programs (advisory boards, reference account development),
   - content management,
   - marketing operations,
   - public relations,
   - analyst relations,
   - field marketing (if applicable),
   - brand advertising,
   - online marketing,
   - internal communications,

I am surprised by the number of CMOs who are expected to invest a percentage of their time in innovation, yet they fail to create an "innovation reserves" category in their annual budget. One CMO for a $2.5B firm whom I recently met does not have any such budget category. Consequently, whenever he wants to experiment with a new social media campaign or field marketing program, he is forced to withdraw those funds from his existing brand advertising budget. For companies that do not command the number one position among competitors, this can be a damaging to the brand and ultimately render their marketing initiatives stale.

4. Balance savings discussions with spending discussions. Have you ever benchmarked your agency and research investments against industry standards? How do you know whether you are spending too much for these services? In one instance, McKinsey & Company reported that a consumer packaged-goods company conducted a study of their spend on marketing research and TV commercial testing. They were surprised to learn that they were using more than 48 different marketing research firms, and spending 50 percent more than the industry average on research. Once they made the necessary adjustments, they were able to reallocate 20 percent of their marketing budget to growth initiatives.[9]

5. Create ongoing collaboration opportunities with finance. One CFO from a rapidly growing business to business (B2B) company explains how two different CMOs behaved during planning meetings. The first CMO, whom we will call Barbara, became defensive when he asked for regular updates on her progress against the annual budget. The CFO noticed she was struggling with sticking to the budget, so he assigned a finance staff member ("Eric") to help Barbara with the process. These individuals are often called Financial Planning and Analysis (FP & A) professionals. The CFO told me, "She treated my staff member as if he were beneath her, and exceeded her budget by a large margin. At that point, it felt like a forced marriage."

Shortly after that interchange, Barbara left the company, and a new CMO joined their firm. (Let's call him "Alan.") Within the first few weeks of meeting the CFO, Alan told the CFO, "I want to work with your team to see where every dollar goes. I would like Eric to come to our marketing meetings and help me educate our marketers to be more comfortable with numbers... our top marketing goal is to drive leads to the sales team." This gave the CFO a sense of relief and a greater commitment to marketing than he previously had.

Former Amazon Fashion Director of HR, Val Wright, shared a shining example of how CFOs and CMOs collaborate successfully. She is currently the president of Val Wright Consulting in Los Angeles, California. "Our leadership team knew in order to educate and inspire customers to buy fashion on Amazon.com, we had to invest heavily in marketing, which was an alien concept at Amazon. We also had to hire different expertise in the marketing team to realize this vision and reward different behaviors." That's when, in 2011, she reveled in the opportunity to join Amazon. "My role was to identify and attract employees and build a leadership plan that would deliver the strategy."[10]

Wright knew that this launch would not be an easy task. At the time, upscale fashion was not in Amazon's wheelhouse. They were known for selling inexpensive, low-quality clothing necessities. To prove their commitment to gaining a foothold in this sector, Amazon accomplished several strategy coups—all within a couple of years: they hired a former Gap executive, Cathy Beaudoin, as president to help elevate the Amazon Fashion brand; they launched MyHabit (a Gilt and RueLaLa flash sale competitor); and they acquired Zappos.

Wright participated in the early executive team discussions to formulate the growth strategy. "Decisions were made on data, and in meetings it was perfectly acceptable to challenge existing models, marketing plans, and approaches. 'Debate and decide' is one of the famous core values at Amazon. Once the decisions are made, you have to commit and move on. The CMO and the CFO worked in tandem to identify the investment and metrics for success, so when we all sat in our annual strategy review session with Jeff Bezos and the Amazon Executive Team, we were aligned, clear on the details and data along with the positive impact on the customer experience."[11] She attributes much of that success to an open relationship between the CFO, Kevin Gasper, and CMO, Jenny Perry.

In Table 17.1, Patterson has developed a succinct checklist of financial blind spots that every CFO needs to uncover and address. Mindful marketers are aware of their peers' concerns, and can contribute to the conversation to transform them. This is true whether you are a start-up or an online juggernaut like Amazon.

Table 17.1 How Does Your Business Stack Up?

Here are five of the most common core areas in which we find financial blind spot opportunities and risks. Improve your information accuracy, and therefore business decisions and profitability, by turning these negatives into positives:

1. My business is unsure who its 10 most profitable customers are.
2. My business occasionally capitalizes expenses that had created an asset with what now may be a questionable recorded value.
3. My business does not know how changes at one of our top 10 customers may affect our bottom line.
4. My business isn't yet looking into an asset that it will be better off selling at a loss to free up cash to pursue a more promising opportunity.
5. My business paints an overly optimistic picture of itself to a customer, vendor, or financing source.[12]

Copyright © 2012 Gary Patterson, used with permission

An articulate marketing leader is a confident marketing leader. By learning the language of finance and marketing planning, you will bring a smile to the CFO's face and earn the most coveted award: their confidence.

> **INNER MARKETING GURU Inquiry #17:**
>
> What is the best strategy for my team to earn the CFO's trust and confidence?

This page intentionally left blank

CHAPTER 18

THE CMO AND THE CIO: CROSSING THE RAGING RIVER

Peace cannot be kept by force. It can only be achieved by understanding.
—Albert Einstein

Did you hear the one about the two monks? Here is author David Gerrold's version of the fable:

> One day, the two monks arrived at a deep river. At the edge of the river, a young woman sat weeping, because she was afraid to cross the river without help. She begged the two monks to help her. The younger monk turned his back. The members of their order were forbidden to touch a woman.
> But the older monk picked up the woman without a word and carried her across the river...and continued his journey. The younger monk came after him, scolding him and berating him for breaking his vows...
> Finally, at the end of the day the older monk turned to the younger one. "I only carried her across the river. You have been carrying her all day." [1]

Marketing's perception of information technology (IT) is a contemporary, cautious tale of two monks: one monk wants to scold the other, and one is ready to let go of the past and move forward. As you refer to the images in Figure 18.1, Which monk are you? And how much is it

Figure 18.1 Which Monk Are You?

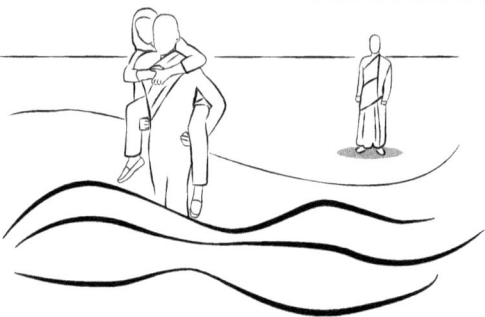

Courtesy of graphic illustrator Toni Glover.

holding you back in your ability to create breakthrough sales, innovations, and customer experiences?

If you are the IT executive, you may still be carrying that woman across the metaphorical river. IT executives can point to countless examples over the past 40 years, where rogue departments have excluded IT from strategic activities, only to see their data get lost, corrupted, or shared with competitors. Jerry Grochow, a seasoned technology consultant and former vice president of information technology at Massachusetts Institute of Technology, reminds us of the history of user activities that date back to the 1980s:

> When Lotus and Excel spreadsheets were invented, they were considered the greatest thing since sliced bread by the finance department. IT saw them differently—they were renegade systems that were slowly becoming integral to the company's operation. They had no controls. I recall myriad stories where "Sally," the finance manager, retired, and she was the only person who knew how to use the spreadsheets. IT was called in to fix the problem.[2]

Today, CIOs are looking at the growth in predictive analytics, mobile, and cloud computing from a historical perspective. Some are concerned that history may be repeating itself. Grochow wonders, "Will we have a bunch of marketing folks who will call us when it's too late, when things go awry? Forward-thinking CIOs are trying to get ahead of this. They want to be involved early in the ideation process, and shift user perceptions that 'IT is not very responsive.'"[3]

The CIO is facing an equal number of pressures as the marketing organization. In essence, they are the key executive responsible for the company's technological infrastructure. In theory, CIOs are expected to dedicate their time to understanding the corporate strategic direction. Effective CIOs help with formulating as well as deploying programs that support that strategic direction. Communications capacity, security, storage, networking, website, vendor relations, IT staffing, stewardship of customer and financial data, and other functions fall squarely in their wheelhouse.

While IT spends the majority of its time invested in internal areas, Marketing spends their time on external market drivers. That is where they can either become perfect allies or adversaries. If marketing continually crosses the raging river of IT discontent, and fails to find the areas of common ground, they may blame it on these areas:

- *Marketers and IT groups work in different "time zones."* Customers, who often operate at warp speed, expect their vendors to deliver at the same pace. This forces Product Development, Marketing, Sales, and Customer Cervice to manage a high level of service expectations. Since 2011, Forrester Research has been tracking the perceptions that IT and Marketing share about each other, and they report that "IT often overlooks the intensity of the pace of customers' demands, which marketing confronts daily. As a result, it's no surprise that marketing and IT come to the table with vastly different organizations and skills.... Misalignment in communication of strategic priorities persists.... IT is more confident that it understands marketing's priorities (68%), whereas marketing is less confident (49%) in its ability to communicate IT's priorities. The nearly 20-percentage-point difference highlights marketing's need to better understand IT's mind-set and more fully communicate its priorities to IT."[4] These disparate perceptions also lead to different perceptions of what priorities need attention, and how urgently.
- *IT lags at bolstering its own marketing expertise.* Forrester's report says that "close to half of IT leaders (49%) believe that 'the CIO hires staff with marketing expertise,' but only 19% of marketing leaders (agree)."[5]

    Hiring IT professionals with marketing skills not only receives one of the lowest-scoring responses from marketers but also represents the largest disparity between IT and marketing execs' perspectives. The 30-percentage-point difference in perception demonstrates the root cause of marketing and IT misalignment—the lack of marketing expertise and knowledge on the technology side of the house."[6]

- *IT's historical* raison d'être *and budget are project driven, not strategy driven.* Wayne McKinnon, founder of The McKinnon Group, asserts that "the CIO position is usually filled with a person possessing a stronger background in technology rather than business. Among the IT circles that I frequent, this comment is blasphemous, but I stand by that remark. In half of the companies whom I have advised, I have found that CIOs are no longer invited to the executive roundtable meetings. In these organizations, the title 'CIO' is just a title, and it really means IT manager."[7]

Some companies are skipping IT altogether during the budget planning cycle, and allocating budget directly to Marketing. Patrick Gray, a blogger with *ZDNet*, cautions technology readers that Marketing is taking on a broader set of IT budget responsibility. "While IT spending for major ERP and supply-chain initiatives has largely become a thing of the past, Marketing is emerging as a major technology buyer. Marketing has become deeply dependent on technology as its tasks have shifted from major mass-marketing campaigns to highly tailored, data-driven 'engagements' that occur continually. It's worth taking some time to understand the trends in marketing and sitting down with the CMO, since he or she may ultimately be setting the IT agenda in 2014."[8]

Expectations on CIOs have changed forever. Some will adapt and explore unchartered waters; others will remain safely on the shore. Gray finds that "the availability of managed services and the viability of lights-out IT make a purely utility-oriented CIO increasingly irrelevant. The days of striving for high uptime numbers are now an expectation rather than a cause for recognition, and increasingly complex technologies like big data build a case for hiring outside expertise and bypassing internal IT directly. Consider how your IT department and the CIO are perceived by your peers. Are you the technical plumber called in to connect the dots after the key strategic decisions have been made, or are you a trusted source of guidance and insight that helps to shape your company's future?"[9]

Change is happening to help close the gap between IT and Marketing. Forrester noticed an upswing in areas where IT and Marketing leaders align and agree. Their 2013 survey revealed that "More than three-fourths (78%) of marketing leaders and 81% of IT leaders agree that 'customer intelligence is a strategic priority for [their] company.'"[10] Furthermore, they have witnessed an increase in commitment to three key practices: joint/shared ownership of marketing technology projects, communal steering committees to review and sign off on projects for marketing that require technology, and a mutually acceptable meeting cadence. These steps help both groups speak the same language and agree on the rate of process and industry change they are willing to absorb.

I find these collaborative processes exciting, because they make it easier for marketers *and* CIOs to compare notes on what they are learning from customers. My CMO clients are now working on initiatives to create "one view of the truth" (a single view of the customer), build standard content marketing platforms that align with how customers buy, and drive actionable insights derived from reliable customer intelligence and predictive lead scoring models. None of this can succeed without everyone investing time with customers.

These practices offer a long-term benefit as well: they help both teams play a more proactive versus reactive role in selecting the best enabling technology. When both groups are involved in the early stage of technology evaluation, neither department cares who owns the budget. They care about what's best for the customer and the business.

At technology solutions provider Dell, CMO Karen Quintos shares that single customer focus with the Global CIO, Adriana "Andi" Karaboutis. When they began working together in 2011, Quintos expected that they would be spending most of their time talking about security, privacy, and budget. Instead, "what came up was: how do we align your priorities to our customers' and employees' needs? Frankly, the company owns the budget, and I don't care. The question we kept asking was, 'Who is going to shepherd the customer experience?'"[11]

Marketing and IT can thrive as allies, especially since external forces influence their mutual kismet. When they collectively acknowledge these forces and use them to inform their initiatives, they can create strategies that their respective organizations will wholeheartedly commit to launching:

- Organizations are rapidly shifting their internal IT support to software-as-a-service, or "3rd platform" support. According to the International Data Corporation (IDC), the adoption of these technologies—such as Customer Relationship Management, marketing automation, and customer experience programs—will redefine 90% of IT roles.[12] Marketing will suddenly own budget for IT innovations they may barely understand. In order to succeed, they will need to hire talent for skills that are unproven and ill-defined. Data scientists, sales experts, and demand generation experts represent today's nascent professions. Fred Magee, adjunct research adviser with IDC's Research Network, also predicts that "by 2017, the transfer of 3rd Platform investments from IT to line-of-business budgets will require 60% of CIOs to reduce the cost of infrastructure and operations."[13]

- The beat of the "young and mobile" drum will get louder. Young IT professionals and marketers who have had experience working in both areas will increasingly influence strategic marketing and customer experience initiatives. How will traditional industries, such as banking, bricks and mortar retail, and education securely and safely link their capabilities to Facebook, Instagram, Snapchat, or Pinterest? These could just become the future default browsers on tomorrow's mobile devices. Young savvy users may demand it.
- The 24 x 7 "need for customer speed" is here to stay. CIOs recognize that focusing on internal cost controls and operations has great value, but it represents a 1990s approach to IT leadership. They need to step forward and lead discussions that germinate the next innovation that will improve their customers' conditions. They also need to allocate a portion of their time to attending customer events and trade shows, as well as participating in sales calls. These activities inform them as to how their initiatives accelerate growth.
- CIOs have to pick up the pace with building these customer-centric superpowers, or they may get stuck in the 1990s. In *CIO's* annual State of the CIO survey, which was released in December 2013, Kim Nash writes that "25 percent of the 722 CIOs we surveyed report that the IT group is perceived by colleagues as a true business peer—or even a game-changer—that can create and launch new products and open new markets."[14]

Mindful marketers can establish powerful bridges with IT teams and the CIO by following four pilotage principles: *collaboration, customer focus, compassion,* and *candor.* These ways of being are transformative first steps in building those bridges:

1. *Establish collaboration protocols.*

When IT and Marketing can approach initiatives using the same framework and language, collaboration happens more naturally. McKinnon has designed a top-down model in Figure 18.2 to guide strategic discussions and, over time, close the gap between what Marketing *wants*, and what IT *delivers*.[15]

Figure 18.2 Table McKinnon

Closing the Gap Between What Marketing Wants and What IT Delivers		
Objective	**Sample activities**	**People to involve**
Level 4: Establish Marketing strategy and business outcomes	Determine business objectives	Marketing's internal customers
	Identify leading and trailing indicators of business improvement	Marketing team
Level 3: Identify tactics to achieve those outcomes	Explore online and offline methods as well as internal (IT) and external (service provider) services	Marketing team
		Technology visionaries (IT or other)
		CIO representative / IT Business Relationship Manager
Level 2: Identify service requirements and high level service design	Determine data security and customer exposure considerations	Marketing representatives
	Identify service levels (e.g. hours of availability, customer support response times, performance, transaction volumes, etc.)	IT Business relationship manager/Service Level Manager (IT)
		Subject matter experts (IT)
Level 1: Determine IT resources and technical aspects Perform the technical work	Select proprietary tools or "off the shelf" options that meet the requirements Implement the solution	Business relationship manager (IT)
		Service Level Manager IT
		Technical specialists (IT)

© Wayne McKinnon 2014. All rights reserved.

While this framework may appear simple, it is not easy to implement. McKinnon says, "It is particularly useful in preventing both teams from jumping to technical solutions without properly exploring important options at all four levels. The traditional conversation around the IT department gathering requirements from the Marketing department often focuses on the technical requirements, not the business requirements. Often, when marketing speaks of business results, that part of the conversation is lost on many IT practitioners. They zone out until they can turn the conversation back to a discussion of technology."

"Meanwhile, marketing walks out of the design meeting assuming that IT has things well in hand. In reality, neither party ends up focusing on what it takes to deliver business results. Certainly there are exceptions to this bad behavior."

In summary, McKinnon reminds us that "it's not about the technology and how you are going to use it. It's about what marketing is trying to achieve, and which technologies support that. "This 'Closing the Gap' model helps both sides recognize that they are often talking about two different things when they address business imperatives." [16]

2. *Agree on how you will collect, analyze, and take action on customer data.*

In 2012, Quintos determined that a creating single view of Dell's fifty million customers was a big bet worth making. Quintos reached out to CIO Karaboutis to take inventory of their marketing analytics tools across their 180 markets across the globe. "What we found was that you have to pick a few tools, pivot where you want to go, and turn data into insights and action. Between my team and Andi's team, we have built a strong digital analytics platform that allows us to link customer, partner, digital, and sales data. We integrate it in a way that allows one view of the customer. We can now turn that into personalized, one on one programs for each customer."[17] Not only has Karaboutis been successful at supporting one version of Eloqua across these diverse markets, but she and her team have also helped Dell's marketing and sales teams integrate Eloqua with Salesforce.

3. *Be compassionate.* Compassion starts with understanding the recurring pressures that most CIOs are facing—and

recognizing that some of these pressures are the same ones that Marketing must address. That may not be the case today, but it will be in the future. The mantra "United we stand, divided we fall" rings true for today's CIO-CMO alliance.

Consider these realities as you position your new initiatives with IT:

- The rate of change will only increase, and their headcount usually will not.
- Ongoing pressure to reduce IT costs will not ease, even while IT leaders are expected to be innovation leaders.
- Cybersecurity and privacy threats undermine, if not sabotage, every initiative or legacy program.
- IT leaders face a barrage of compliance and reporting requirements, even though they were supposedly hired to create competitive advantage through breakthrough systems and technology.
- They are expected to deliver quickly and reliably, even though they are not in control of the underlying cloud-based and outsourced platforms.

4. *Make candor your rallying cry.* Quintos and Karaboutis agreed to discuss a few core areas, such as integration and talent, without caring who got credit. They are both very clear about Dell's strategic priorities, and are not afraid to address sensitive resource issues in the process. Over the past few years, Dell's acquisition strategy helped them grow more rapidly, and both executives were clear on the urgent need to make those integrations successful and swift. Quintos shared that "as we made acquisitions (they averaged eight per year since 2011), we found that almost every new company was focused on demand generation. Our ability to take what was a really good marketing organization and tie it to the Dell brand and base of 50 million customers was critical."[18]

Second, they continually review the talent profiles of their teams. Quintos found that "In some parts of marketing, the talent profiles have changed. We have hired individuals who are data scientists—and they are really hard to find. At the same time, Andi is hiring people who understand marketing. Andi has hired a Chief Digital Officer that sits on the staff with my head of operations and tools. We have invested in that function because we need a consistent approach to our digital strategy. Decision science is in demand."[19]

The past is the past. IT cannot linger on its past mistakes and grievances with Marketing, and Marketing with IT. The secret to long-term success between IT and Marketing lies in their selfless commitment to the organization mission. As they embark on that journey, CIOs and CMOs must ensure there's room for two rowers in the boat. Together, they can safely cross any raging river.

> **INNER MARKETING GURU Inquiry #18:**
>
> What market imperatives require proactive, joint collaboration with our IT counterparts?

CHAPTER 19

SALES AND MARKETING: RETHINKING THE SYSTEM

"A monk asked Master Joshu, "I have just entered this monastery. I beg you, Master, please give me instructions." Joshu asked, "Have you eaten your rice gruel yet?" The monk answered, "Yes, I have." Joshu said, "Then wash your bowls."
—C. Ts-ung-jung lu, Koan #39,
from E. Book of Serenity

One of the greatest teachers of our era, the late Dr. Martin Luther King, understood how specific actions and behaviors within a broader context are connected. When he was confronted by racists, King recognized how their behaviors, and a single action, related to the scourge of racism. Many historians believe he was a systems thinker. To this day, his leadership provides a lesson—and a cautionary tale—to both marketers and sales professionals.

While seated on the stage at the 1962 Southern Christian Leadership Conference, King was accosted by a white Nazi, who punched him several times in the face. While people rushed to his aid, King calmly responded that he would not press charges. He was quoted about this incident later in his biography *Martin Luther King on Leadership*: "The system that we live under creates people such as this youth. I am not interested in pressing charges. I'm interested in changing the kind of system that produces this kind of man."[1]

What kind of organizations are we creating with today's sales systems and approaches? In my opinion, we are unwittingly designing revenue-hungry, metrics-obsessed teams who are often focused on short-term outcomes.

Many experts want us to believe that improving revenue performance should be the number one priority for both sales and marketing leaders, and that both groups need to operate from the same instruction manual. They encourage VPs of Sales and CMOs to agree on the ideal strategies for demand creation, sales enablement, account management, content management, and compensation systems. However, managing solely by the numbers may make managers look good, but does not foster great leaders. The great marketing and sales leaders additionally focus on the *customer conversations, behaviors,* and *environments* that will drive the results.

As we discuss the root causes of sales and marketing dissonance, it helps to apply a systems thinking approach. In 1956, Professor Jay Forrester founded the Systems Dynamic Group at Massachusetts Institute of Technology's Sloan School of Management and introduced systems thinking. Today, countless institutions use it to promote understanding of complex topics and issues, such as politics, the environment, medicine, education, organizational change, and societal trends. Using this approach, sales and marketing may view their roles and relationships from a broader, more integrated perspective.

The systems thinking approach contrasts with traditional analysis, which studies systems by breaking them down into their separate elements. In lieu of analyzing the most common "parts" of sales and marketing interplay, let's take a broader view and search for the root cause of dissonance:

- Sales and marketing overinvest in business processes at the expense of connecting with their customers. Tim Riesterer, CMO of training company Corporate Visions, says, "When people talk about sales and marketing alignment, they usually start with demand generation and qualified leads. In other words, marketing creates materials to help foster leads, and salespeople have conversations with the leads. But what they're forgetting is the thing people should actually *say* when they engage a prospect. It's about the message and the story. With the ever-increasing amount of data on prospects and customers, marketers and salespeople need to be able to align and translate that data into a compelling story to help overcome the status quo barrier with the prospect."[2]

I concur with Riesterer. When I used to carry a revenue quota, my competitive landscape was peppered with a handful of companies—as well as the prospect's own bias to maintain status quo. If I could not appeal to the buyer's personal self-interest and create an urgency to change, that buyer would seldom move forward and buy anything. The status quo is the default setting for most humans. Our Inner Marketing Guru understands this and doesn't try to change the buyer. Instead, they ask permission to debate, expand their thinking, and show them the short- and long-term implications of business as usual.

- *Internal systems are not keeping up with changing customer behaviors.* Michael Ni, CMO and Senior VP of Marketing and Products at Avangate, says that "customers have become savvier—they transact via more touch points (online, social, mobile, in-app, call center, direct sales, and resellers) than ever before, and they do far more research. Sometimes, they are better informed than a vendor's sales teams. Today, B2C [business-to-consumer] and B2B [business-to-business] customer behavior have converged into what we call B2i (Business to individual). B2i customers expect pricing transparency and purchasing on their own terms, a shift that is putting more pressure on marketing teams to act like sales."[3] Showrooming, a customer practice that now guides many retail purchases, and the abundance of online research, have forever transformed how buyers buy and how companies enable the process.
- Consensus decision-making is becoming de rigueur with buyers for big ticket purchases. I have noticed, particularly over the past five years, that senior corporate executives are unwilling to make as many bold moves without conferring with their teams. They seek buy-in before they will announce a strategic initiative, often causing unnecessary delays and missed opportunities to be first to market. Just when salespeople think they have a strong inside supporter, the buyer will ask them to present the idea to a variety of other stakeholders. Suddenly, the salesperson is engaged in a game of herding cats.

- Customers push more of the initial purchasing risk onto suppliers. Purchasing often wants vendors to accept less payment up front and make subsequent payments contingent on meeting certain milestones.
- The rise of third-party purchasing consultants drives longer sales cycles and undermines effective marketing initiatives. In addition to firms such as Deloitte, BCG, and Accenture, many former employees of vendors are now hanging out their "solopreneur" shingle and helping customers negotiate better deals with vendors.
- The role of sales has diminished in the B2B arena. Today, sales teams are responsible for guiding fewer stages of the buying cycle. Research firms estimate that between 60 percent and 70 percent of the buying decision is completed before a salesperson is allowed to meet the buyer. By that stage, many buyers are nearly ready to negotiate. It's similar to how we buy cars today. We walk into the dealer, armed with competitive quotes, specifications, and consumer reports, and we are ready to negotiate. In cases like these, relationship selling has taken a back seat.
- The cost of attaining true "sales and marketing harmony" can be prohibitive. Within my CMO community, I have not found one marketing organization that operates at optimal levels across every possible discipline. Think of the multitude of moving parts that are essential to optimizing the customer experience. A marketer is expected to oversee several of these areas, some of which did not exist five years ago:
  - marketing automation
  - scoring
  - events planning
  - content creation
  - customer relationship management
  - inside teleprospecting
  - predictive analytics

To exacerbate matters, sales and marketing do not always agree on some key questions to keep the pipeline of leads flowing. For example, who owns what steps within the sales pipeline? What percentage of revenues does marketing own, versus sales? And what are the consequences if marketing sends sales leads and they go stale?

These sources of dissonance have something in common: most are driven by outdated beliefs and behaviors. Due to outdated perceptions of where marketing and sales contribute to company health, Board members and executives continue to ask the wrong question. Most leaders in Western business circles still ask the same old sets of questions during each strategic planning cycle. Once they have established the company's vision, mission, and top priorities, they will typically ask, "What marketing resources, processes and incentives are needed for us to reach this revenue goal?" They proceed to allocate people and funding to attain that "magic number."

With an eye toward systems thinking, let's reframe that question. Is the purpose of a customer-driven company to maximize revenues and profits first, and to nurture lifetime customers second? In mindful, sustainable companies, the purpose is reversed. When you are committed to making a difference and to listening to your Inner Marketing Guru to serve your customers' needs, every resource allocation and incentive decision becomes clearer. In lieu of a "What's in it for us?" philosophy, your company embraces a "What's in it for our customer, so that all will benefit?" philosophy. This is a subtle, yet powerful, shift in how we think about growth and sales and marketing investments. In lieu of a push to drive revenues, a pull strategy, or a magnetic marketing process, evolves.

Marketers can embrace this customer success orientation by implementing these proven recommendations:

1. *Make collaboration your new mantra.* Tim Hill, former president of Global Marketing at education software provider Blackboard, explains the distinctions between average and excellent team alignment:

"Where there is good alignment, it's easier to add more value by working on joint marketing and sales plans, and then measure the impact. When I would walk into the meetings, I knew that people had my back. They were signing off on plans. Win lose or draw, everyone was invested in the outcome."

Where there is poor alignment, I told my executives to key in on the VP of Sales. If we can work together with them and the field salespeople, then alignment will happen from the bottom up. There were many meetings where the GM would lament about marketing—I would then show them examples where the field and the head of sales were successfully implementing the marketing plan. This would neutralize the discussion.

For example, we had two divisions reporting to one president. When I realized there was dysfunction across that division's executive management, sales, and product teams, I approached the president and VP of Product about working together to create a new product. We worked on a free cloud-based app for K–12 school districts that was linked to our emergency notification and antibullying notification service. This could be used by students, parents, school administrators, and bus drivers. It was a big success: we had significant media coverage, an increase in new customer acquisition, and higher retention of current clients. Those executive level alignments, coupled with the launch, were critical to bolstering that division's growth."[4]

2. *Build a Service-Level Agreement (SLA) with the sales team.* Andy Zimmerman, CMO of video technology company Brainshark, worked with the VP of Sales, Larry DiLoreto, to quickly establish a common demand creation process. As he explained, "When Larry joined Brainshark, we quickly established a demand creation system, including definitions of key terminology and stages of the buying cycle and who was accountable for each stage. It can be complex because leads can come from a variety of places: campaigns, existing accounts, resellers, partners and 'bluebirds' (i.e., unexpected sources). Over time, we also created a Sales Enablement Portal which housed our marketing messages, sample presentations, and videos to help our customer-facing teams be much better prepared for sales calls."[5]

Figure 19.1 outlines an SLA that Hill developed with his sales leaders. It served several purposes: it maintained "one view of the truth," streamlined discussions, and defined mutual accountabilities. This

Figure 19.1 Service Level Agreement

Service Level Agreement (SLA) *Example*

Composition of Prospect v. Client Leads
(% of overall leads that should be dedicated to each)

Greenfield Leads	90%
Upsell/Expansion	80%
Total	100%

Marketing Sourced Leads
(% of overall closed sales that are initiated by Marketing and reported in Salesforce)

Historical (Trailing 4 Quarters)	18.0%
Agreed Target for Fiscal Year	25.0%
Annual Marketing Sourced Goal/Target	$2,200,000
Quarterly Marketing Sourced $ Target	$550,000

Estimated Lead Volume Per Sales Rep

	Split by Rep Type	Total Annual Leads by Rep Type	# of Reps	Annual Leads Per Rep	Quarterly Leads Per Rep	Monthly Leads Per Rep
Greenfield	40%	$87	6	98	24	8
Existing Client Leads	60%	$880	8	110	28	9
Total Sales Reps	100%	$967	14	61	15	5

Lead Generation Funnel

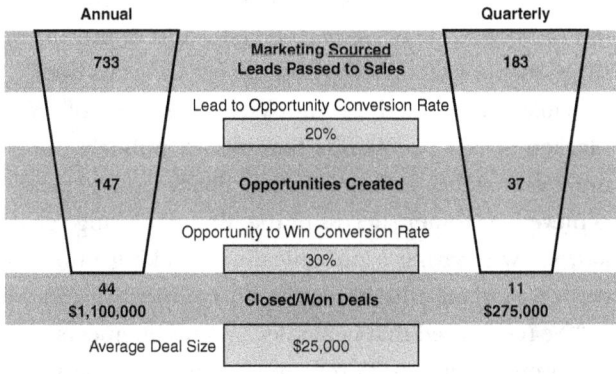

Copyright 2014, Lisa Nirell. All rights reserved.

dashboard, which became a common reference tool, allowed marketing and sales to track three metrics:

- **composition of prospect versus client leads:** the breakdown in the number of leads from new prospects ("greenfield") and existing prospects
- **marketing sourced sales:** the percentage of all closed sales that are initiated by marketing;
- **estimated lead volume by sales representative:** a method to track how many leads each representative was receiving, on average, from marketing. Lead volume, the average close rates from those leads, and the total revenues generated are usually monitored on a monthly, quarterly, and annualized basis.

3. *Dedicate a percentage of your week to sales calls and time with customers.* Many marketers aspire to do this. Unfortunately, they find excuses to revert to activities with which they are more comfortable. When I was a marketing programs manager for BMC Software, I participated in customer executive briefings, online product demonstrations, and customer conference calls. It opened my eyes to how customers spoke and behaved, how they evaluated our company, and what competitors were telling them.

Fortunately, you can find examples of marketers who are unafraid to step out of the familiar and spend time with sales teams and customers. For example, over the past two decades, Greg Jorgensen has remained committed to partnering with sales. This commitment has generated big rewards throughout his career. He is a seasoned CMO and Brand Strategist-in-Residence for technology companies and start-ups.

While he worked as the Vice President of Worldwide Marketing at CrossWorlds Software, a publicly traded technology provider, he noticed that the Sales organization had achieved customer success in the Manufacturing vertical market, yet was having a difficult time breaking into three new vertical markets, which were highly competitive and crowded:

"We recognized that field sales, systems engineers, and inside sales were all taking different approaches to attacking these new market opportunities."[6] Jorgensen and his executive peers had two concerns with their divergent practices. "First, they were not listening deeply to prospects or customers, which included corporate IT system architects, business integration technicians, and C-level executives. They did not clearly understand their individual evolving pain points with using integration software."

"Second, there was increased pressure in the marketplace from competitors claiming product superiority. They were outspending us in marketing and creating confusion among customers. By this stage, executive management was concerned about missing their revenue goals and alienating their customer base."[7]

Jorgensen and his team responded swiftly. They joined sales calls and merged inside sales and marketing teams to get a first-hand appreciation of customer frustrations, sales performance, and messaging disconnects. This helped them determine that their customers and prospects needed to hear a different message: "Instead of promoting single products, our new message would focus on the business and technical benefits of integrating business software applications from the loading dock all the way up to the executive suite and everywhere in-between."

"We also developed a white board sales message that first looked at customer challenges and pain points to help sales teams create a dialogue focused on need, versus leading with product. We redesigned the website around an exchange, which allowed customers, prospects, and partners to test our technology within their own environments against competitive products before they purchased it. This rapidly increased our company visibility and accelerated sales pipeline velocity. Each of these strategies required a team effort, and they helped us to solidify a constant feedback loop."[8]

These alignment efforts reaped dividends. CrossWorld's largest partner, IBM, purchased CrossWorlds Software for between 1.5 and twice annual revenues. Jorgensen noted "it was the only acquisition that IBM had made to date that directly incorporated our existing marketing strategy, sales enablement tools, and go-to-market approaches."[9]

4. *Invite salespeople to marketing brainstorming sessions.* Show them how to facilitate these meetings. This has two benefits: it helps them become increasingly facile with the idea-generation process with their customers and prospects, and it grows their self-esteem. Both skills are essential to helping salespeople apply systems thinking principles to how they sell, and to acting like a peer to their customers. Salespeople who think their primary job is to build friendships with their clients may be liked, but their ideas won't necessarily be respected.

With the dramatic shift in how buyers buy and how marketers think and work, salespeople are feeling an equal amount of performance pressure as their marketing counterparts. What salespeople really need—and where marketers can add value—is in helping sales teams build self-esteem. A paucity of self-esteem is what causes salespeople to say "yes" to every customer request and kowtow to purchasing bullies. These behaviors need to change in today's customer-centric reality.

Healthy companies emerge when sales and marketing are incented to create a customer-centric culture. Marketing fuels this culture by providing the cultural avatars, processes, leads, and tools to sales. When both groups agree to a set of common goals and standards, sales professionals begin to feel like they are part of a purpose greater than getting a commission payment. That is a systems approach that leaders like Martin Luther King would applaud.

> **INNER MARKETING GURU Inquiry #19:**
>
> Where are the greatest gaps between our sales and marketing organizations?

CHAPTER 20

LOOKING INSIDE TO WORK OUTSIDE

We are perishing for lack of fulfillment of our greater needs...we are cut off from the great sources of our inward nourishment and renewal...we must plant ourselves again in the Universe.
—D.H. Lawrence

Among his many talents as a best-selling business author, speaker, and columnist, Marshall Goldsmith, selectively coaches several members of today's elite corporate and military leaders. He is often surprised at the leaders who think they operate differently within their company than outside their company. My favorite story is about one of his challenging coaching clients. Goldsmith says "he was in the 0.1 percentile for treating people with respect.... That means that there were over a thousand people in that company and this person came in dead last. He was hardworking and brilliant; he didn't lie, cheat, or steal. He was just a complete jerk. The case was considered hopeless."

Goldsmith asks, "You know how I helped the guy to change? I asked him, 'How do you treat people at home?' He said, 'Oh, I'm totally different at home.' I said, 'Let's call your wife and kids.' What did his wife say? 'You're a jerk.' Called the kids. 'Jerk.' 'Jerk.' So I said, 'Look, I can't help you make money, you're already making more than God, but do you want to have a funeral that no one attends? Because that's where this train is headed.'"[1]

Who we are being as leaders *within* our organization may not always be consistent with who we are being *outside the four walls* of our organization. By embracing the five mindful marketer qualities that were outlined in chapter 10, you can close those behavioral gaps. This chapter provides some concrete example of how these qualities make a significant difference in how we work with outsiders.

Outsiders can include members from several communities: customers, industry influencers, consultants, associations, and nonprofits. Each group category represents another brand touchstone and another source of referrals. As a refresher, the five qualities of being are:

1. acceptance
2. aliveness
3. articulateness
4. aggregation
5. adaptability

ACCEPTANCE

Acceptance requires that we deeply understand and acknowledge our natural way of operating in the world, and that we set a clear, authentic intention in our marketing. For example, my intention with my marketing is to educate, inspire, and improve my clients' and community's condition. We serve everyone better when we shed ourselves of the exhaustive quest to impress others. Work becomes more joyful.

Jan-Patrick Schmitz, resident and CEO of Montblanc North America, faced a crossroads in the late 1990s—and it was not a joyful moment. Customer preferences suddenly shifted. He and his team needed to swiftly determine how Montblanc would adapt:

"Our distribution changed from mainstream retailers, where our products were historically positioned as a functional item selling for less than $80."[2] Fine stationers started to disappear, and superstores such as OfficeMax and Staples appeared in every shopping center. They started grabbing market share from Montblanc's network of small stationers and boutiques. Schmitz recalls that "Suddenly, our pens became commodities. If we were to continue making pens at the $50–$80 price point, we would not survive."[3]

He quickly organized an off-site planning session to address these threats and begin a long-term brand transformation. "In that meeting, we created a brand map of where we would go next, while also maintaining our roots. We wanted our product to reflect a milestone in your life that you pass down to the next generation. That's when we began the shift from 'Montblanc, the Penmaker' to 'Montblanc, a *maison* offering fine lifetime companions.'" [4]

Montblanc's team realized this would be a long journey to change market perception and choose a new course. They addressed several areas. For example, they agreed to migrate from dominating a single category (pens) to a diversified product portfolio. They also segmented customers away from *pen loving customers* to *luxury goods customers.* Schmitz recalls "countless meetings where a jeweler would ask, 'You are a pen maker, why aren't you working with a stationer?'" We had a specific sequence of what products to launch, and when. We had to be mindful so that we did not lose our existing customers."[5]

Schmitz was painfully aware of the impact on some of their best retailers. "I had countless heartbreaking experiences where some retailers had to close down their stores because they were underperforming, or sales had to call on new stores. I personally went on some of these calls with sales."[6]

On one occasion, Schmitz visited the president of Isetan, one of Japan's largest Japanese retailers. "It took almost four years to convince him of where the brand was going. The store manager toured Montblanc's facility in Germany, and commented on our people's commitment to the new brand. This educational approach worked much more effectively than showing him a Nielsen report."[7]

Schmitz reflects that "we would not have survived as a company if we had not changed. Our top line revenues and our bottom line have multiplied over the past 18 years. The starting price on our luxury pens is now $420, and we are available in over 70 markets."[8]

ALIVENESS

Buddha means "the awakened one" in Sanskrit. Part of the reason for Buddhism's mass appeal is that its central "character," the Buddha, was simply a sentient human being. He was not an angel, a god, nor a person with superpowers worthy of worship. He was a human who chose to abandon the luxurious trappings of living in a palace to seek his own aliveness and enlightenment.

Our own search for aliveness, or enlightenment, can lead us down many unknown paths. Sometimes, that journey forces us to lighten up, to take ourselves less seriously. Self-deprecating humor can play a powerful role in revealing our true selves. That vulnerability allows others to relate to us as peers—as fellow Buddhas.

Peppercomm, an integrated marketing communications firm headquartered in New York, stumbled into their own aliveness through improvisational comedy. Steve Cody and Ed Moed cofounded the firm in 1995. Cody shares how their comedy culture evolved:

> We used to work at J. Walter Thompson. While we acquired some great methods, we witnessed a lot of self-importance, plutocracy, and seriousness. We wanted to create a culture where we could take our clients seriously, but not ourselves. It wasn't until my midlife crisis that I started to perform standup comedy every weekend in hellish locations in the city. As I returned to the office and interacted with younger employees, I noticed that I was becoming more 'in the room.'"[9] Cody added, "In comedy circles, that is code for being a better listener, being mindful."[10]

Over time, Cody refined his craft by performing on weekends. He noticed that his client interactions improved dramatically, so he looked for ways to share these skills with his team. "I invited my comedy coach to attend a Peppercomm management retreat. At the end of a long and contentious day, he arrived—and everyone was nervous. After the 90-minute session, the team said, 'This is lightning in a bottle, and we need to roll this out across our agency.'"[11]

His peers slowly embraced this hipper, edgier, fun approach to working with each other and clients. Today, every Peppercomm employee attends comedy workshops. The partners also began to develop a boundary for what is, and is not, acceptable oral and written workplace vocabulary. Their marketing materials began to reflect an edgier voice that attracted prospective clients in search of this unique, edgy style.

The comedy was contagious. Today, Cody and his colleagues host stand-up comedy fundraisers to help combat autism, leukemia, and lymphoma. Since their humble beginnings two decades ago, they have also earned several industry accolades, including *Crain's NY Business* award in 2012 for the number one "Best Place to Work."

Cody sees an inextricable connection between laughter, mindfulness, and Peppercomm's ability to thrive in a cutthroat industry. "From day one, Ed and I always told employees and clients that, while we took client business very seriously, we did not take ourselves seriously. Stand-up comedy enabled us to ingrain a self-deprecating sense of humor in our culture that actually delivered on that brand promise. Authenticity is the currency in communications nowadays. Our company mantra is *Listen. Engage. Repeat.* It has become part of our DNA and, via publicity, has attracted clients seeking to achieve similar results—whether those results are improved presentation skills, an enhanced culture, or both."[12]

Improvisational comedy also builds our confidence in sharing new ideas with others, even when our inner voice says it could be a wrong or crazy idea. Freelance writer Lisa Evans recently reported on the benefits of improvisation in *FastCompany*: "An improvisation technique [author and comedian] Connolly often employs is a word toss in which one person says a word and the next person says a word that is inspired by the previous word. 'Most of the time, people will listen to everyone else except the person directly before them,' he laughs. 'The reason is they're thinking about what they're going to say and they're not focused on what other people are saying.' This exercise teaches the importance not only of listening but understanding the other's point of view before reacting.'"[13] Perhaps there is a reason why Buddha is often seen laughing in ancient etchings—he may have been one of the earliest improv performers, as seen in figure 20.1.

Figure 20.1 Was Buddha One of the Early Improv Performers?

Courtesy of graphic illustrator Toni Glover.

ARTICULATENESS

This mindful quality could mean the difference between market triumph and market obsolescence. Being articulate can be even more challenging when a company hires outside advisers to design, launch, or manage an initiative. In 2013, The Standish Group recounted that 61 percent of consulting projects either fail to deliver the value they should or are challenged. This is only a 2 percent improvement in projects over 2010. Clearly, our unlimited access to big data and slick multimedia presentation tools does not always bolster project success rates.[14]

My experience shows that the primary cause of these failures is the inability of the executive sponsor to persuasively communicate expectations—specifically, joint accountabilities, business objectives, and success measures.

The probability of ongoing failures remains high. After several years of cost-cutting and shoestring budgets, CEOs and boards are reinvesting in myriad strategic projects requiring outside experts. They require help with exploring and pursuing new markets, leveraging information technology (IT) to align marketing and sales programs, and using big data to reach more customers, personalize customer interactions, predict customer buying preferences, and nurture existing customers.

David Fields, the founder of advisory firm Ascendant Consortium and author of *The Executive's Guide to Consultants*, helps Fortune 500 companies optimize their investment and experience with consultants and find great outside partners. He has found that the biggest trap that companies fall into when evaluating consultants is when they search for *situation* instead of *outcome* expertise.

Fields explains that "it's tempting for a marketer to look for a data scientist who has experience applying big data in their specific industry. That is called *situation expertise*, and it is the wrong profile to guide your search. Instead, look for someone who has *outcome-based expertise*. They may have driven a measureable increase in qualified leads, account retention, or product sales where big data was used. Someone who has done this is a better fit for your objective."[15]

Companies also struggle when they forget to structure the project properly up front to mitigate mutual risk. This is another example where a lack of clear communication contributes to a higher likeliness of failure. The three most common areas of risk could include

- internal client risks (the internal stakeholders may not buy into the change introduced, your company is acquired, or you change strategy);
- consultant risks (the project approach fails, the lead partner resigns);
- exogenous risks (one of the client's competitors does something unexpected, the price of raw materials skyrockets, a key supplier goes out of business, or a government agency imposes a fine on the client).

Here are some things to include in your advisory agreement to minimize risk:

1. *Start with the "Why."* When embarking on a new initiative that includes consultants, ask your team to reach common responses to these questions (which Fields refers to as the Context Document):
    - What is the situation that is leading us to bring in an outside expert or agency?
    - What are our desired business outcomes? How will we be better off when it is completed?
    - What are our indicators of success?
    - What are the risks in this project? (internal, expert and exogenous)?
    - What is the value of taking on this project?
    - What parameters will limit or affect the project?[16]
2. *Reduce mutual risk by including a knowledge transfer option in the agreement.* For instance, a consultant can offer some level of ongoing mentoring to the client organization. This fosters self-sufficiency and collaboration.
3. *Include an option in the agreement that allows the consultant to schedule a vacation.* In exchange, the consultant can better accommodate the client and manage their other commitments. This is how partners work effectively.
4. *Ask the consultant to absorb a percentage of the project risk.* For example, agree to pay half of the fees in advance and promise to pay a bonus if the project milestones are met or exceeded.[17]

These articulate options move leaders one step closer to creating a winning collaboration.

AGGREGATION

A strategic marketing leader gains inspiration and insights from disparate sources. I consider natural curiosity of the world around us as a safeguard against corporate navel-gazing. Influencer relationships, for example, can be as powerful and fruitful as the relationships you have with your customers. Think of the authors, bloggers, industry analysts, and subject matter experts who can make or break your reputation with just one blog post. Sometimes these outsiders appear from unknown places and can destroy or bolster your brand.

Sandy Katz, a seasoned VP of Sales and Marketing, mitigated the risk of losing market credibility by designing an influencer strategy in two of his previous positions. "We built relationships with influencers (key opinion leaders) with the explicit goal of legitimizing our categories. In both companies, the category was new to most of the world. It created skepticism, tough questions and, not surprisingly, a great deal of misinformation from competitors and other experts whose reputation was built on existing products."[18]

He recalls his experience as both VP of the Consumer Group and CMO at GOJO Industries, where he helped to launch Purell, a top-selling hand sanitizer. Purell was not an overnight success—although the product was created in 1988, it took two decades to gain market acceptance and to legitimize an entirely new product category. "Fortunately, there was a growing stable of sound research and a few experts who saw the wisdom. Eventually obtaining the Center for Disease Control's recommendation for the healthcare industry stating that alcohol-based hand sanitizers should be the first line of hand hygiene used in lieu of soap and water was a huge category validator. We worked with a few industry experts such as Dr. Alan Greene, Dr. Gerba (aka "Dr. Germ"), and the National Consumer League to help us spread the word and refute misinformation."[19]

He was not completely sure the influencer strategy would work. "At first it felt like it might not take hold, but then there was a tipping point. All of a sudden, everyone was talking about it. Our growth would have been much slower, and we probably would not have reached the level of acceptance we reached. Studies are one thing, but hearing it directly from a respected expert carries a lot of weight."[20]

Katz's track record for reaching out to a wide range of influencers, and his natural ability to seek input from diverse sources, has served him well in his 30-year marketing career.

ADAPTABILITY

I have always loved the aphorism "Life is what happens when you are busy making other plans." Our ability to swiftly shift gears during times of change and seize new, more enriching opportunities reflects the quality of an effective marketing leader. Sometimes, your customers push you in new directions without warning.

In 2010, when Chris Pick became CMO of Apptio, a technology business management (TBM) software company, he realized that IT leaders were facing the risk of becoming irrelevant. If the trend continued, he believed that "CIOs would be seen simply as keeping the lights on, instead of driving change and innovation within IT."[21] Pick and his Apptio colleagues were committed to creating an entirely new category of technology—one that did not yet have major competitors or a community of followers to help CIOs effectively manage IT. "We found this threat facing CIOs across every industry. And we had a solution in mind: to help CIOs run IT like every other business. Our CIO customers saw another solution. They viewed it as a new discipline that required professional standards and an association to support its development."[22]

Pick and his team pondered the benefits of hosting some small peer discussions. "In 2007, we brought together six CIOs from different industries: Cisco, First American, DirecTV, and Clorox were part of the group. Their regular meetings evolved into an advisory council to Apptio, and they shared best practices. Apptio listened to their challenges, and began to build their TBM software platform to fit those needs."

Pick observed that "the CIOs experienced an immediate benefit: they pioneered a new category (TBM) to provide answers to the difficult problems they were trying to solve. TBM helped Apptio by giving us a platform to stand on, and it was as credible as the CIOs who helped create it."[23] Within a few years, Pick "watched this grow into a robust community. We formalized it—we invited more CIOs to regularly meet via online telepresence, and in 2010, we hosted the first TBM Summit. This event grew and gave rise to a full-time nonprofit called the TBM Council. This new group of IT leaders continues to grow today with academic partnerships, expansion into Europe and research initiatives. Today, the Council has 1,100 members."[24]

Today, if you were to rate your level of mastery in these five areas, what would you discover? You don't have to wait until your family calls you a jerk to improve. Find inspiration from these mindful marketers and see what shifts happen. If you begin laughing out loud, you are probably on the right track.

INNER MARKETING GURU Inquiry #20:

What mindful qualities can we bring to our relationships with outside firms and colleagues?

CHAPTER 21

STARTING THE REVOLUTION

Do not go where the path may lead, go instead where there is no path and leave a trail.

—Ralph Waldo Emerson

If you have progressed this far into this book, chances are high that you have taken the time to reflect on how you can introduce mindful approaches and strategies within your organization. The five qualities we have discussed—acceptance, aliveness, articulateness, aggregation, and adaptability—are simple, but they may not always be easy to deploy.

The ability to successfully introduce these qualities depends on two factors: your commitment to living a mindful life (You don't have a "personal life" and a "professional life," you have one life); and your organization's willingness to participate in the mindful revolution.

HOW REVOLUTIONARIES ARE BORN

Let's assume you have made that mindfulness commitment to yourself, your family, and your team. You are "all in." Then comes the tougher part: getting support from your boss, CEO, or board. You will need a compelling business trend or event to fuel your revolution. These are common scenarios to consider as you craft your call to action:

1. Your company is preparing for a merger or acquisition.
2. You have just joined a new organization, and are expected to raise the performance bar.

3. You need to scale your business in order to grow more quickly.
4. The economic buyers within your key customer accounts (CIO, CFO, VP of Sales, CEO, or others) tell you that your messages (or your sales teams' approaches) are not resonating with them.
5. You are entering a new market that operates and thinks differently from your traditional markets.
6. Economic and buyer behavioral shifts are causing you to reorganize your marketing and sales teams.
7. Your highest-performing team member recently resigned, and you are completely under resourced.
8. Your customers are complaining about the time it takes to get a response or to fulfill a request.
9. You recently lost a few significant sales opportunities, from ostensibly perfect prospects, to a key competitor.
10. Your website is perceived by influencers and customers as a static, online brochure.

The financial and emotional commitment from your executive team or board is a significant accomplishment. Once you have identified that compelling business event, it's up to you to determine what initiative will be the platform that sparks the revolution. My clients have, for example, launched a customer reference program, a lead scoring system using predictive analytics, an inbound marketing system, a rebranding initiative, or a Customer Advisory Board. Others have introduced the community manager concept to their organization, where one person (or team) becomes the listening post and the customer engagement expert across all channels. The container within which you express this mindful way of being is a jumping-off point where you can test and learn from your experiences.

Not so fast. You still have one more step to complete. You first need to determine where you are before you can determine where you are going. Otherwise, you could be jumping across a dangerously deep and wide canyon instead of a gulley.

When I work with clients who are facing these pivot points, I ask them to assess their current state before they make any organization-wide announcements about the initiative. As I mentioned, a pivot point can naturally occur when a new executive is assigned to a team or role (such as a CMO). That new executive will usually review the current state to assess what is working, what is not working, and how the informal communications channels are in play. In order to determine an organization's readiness and willingness to change, the executive must assess four areas, which I outlined in the Performance Accelerant Model™ in chapter 13:

1. internal stakeholder team
2. executive sponsorship team
3. customers
4. current culture

My clients often ask for my help in gathering anonymous, candid input from these four categories. Some CEOs and marketing leaders recognize that they will never hear the hard truths from constituents if they ask these questions without additional validation. It is natural for some stakeholders to be fearful of upsetting the status quo. They will only tell that leader what she wants to hear, or agree with her preexisting perceptions. Every participant needs to feel safe in sharing their insights without fear of retribution.

I also discourage company leaders from distributing an online survey or hosting focus groups, then amassing the cloaked responses. This is an example where big data can create big disappointments.

First, these surveys will not capture the tone of voice, the sidebar comments, nor the rich, spontaneous conversations. You will find the same limitations if you host group webinars, town hall meetings, and conference calls. They are simply too impersonal. Don't waste your time unless you are gathering data to support your initial set of firsthand responses.

Secondly, surveys impede you from uncovering resistance to your revolutionary initiatives. In any change initiative, you want to encourage this resistance early in the cycle, versus once the initiative has launched. While some people pride themselves in being web trolls, and use the Web to disparage ideas and people, most professionals do not fit this description. They want a safe forum in which to be heard and understood. Engage them in these discussions as soon as you can and prove that you are serious about fostering a collaborative, transparent culture.

Investing just a few weeks to gather this baseline information using face-to-face and live phone conversations will reap more accurate results than a technology-driven approach. In the worst-case scenario, you will quickly recognize whether your culture can support a customer-centric, transparent, and mindful approach to marketing.

A MINDFUL REVOLUTIONARY

Marketing revolutionary Jascha Kaykas-Wolff provides a contemporary example of a mindful marketer. He joined Mindjet as the CMO in 2011 to help reshape the company's brand and accelerate their current growth rate. He immediately began interviewing the executive team, customers, and marketing colleagues to assess Mindjet's strengths and culture.

Through a series of interviews, and consistent with company strategy, he was able to confirm that "we needed to shift our company positioning from individual mind mapping solutions to project and team task management. The marketing organization had a group of very capable contributors, but the organizational structure and business processes used to launch projects were not set up to move quickly through a repositioning exercise. Several years earlier, when I had worked within Microsoft's Online Services Group, I observed that the traditional "waterfall" software development process was not allowing the development teams to respond quickly enough to customer input for web-based products. It didn't make sense to make quarterly product changes when customers were providing feedback every day."[1]

The "waterfall" model involves distinct, sequential steps such as requirements gathering, design, implementation, verification/quality assurance, and maintenance, and it no longer served this division of Microsoft. "Our marketing organization at Mindjet, when I first joined, operated analogous to the engineering teams at Microsoft during my tenure there. As we embarked on the repositioning, we began implementing agile marketing processes at Mindjet."[2]

Unlike waterfall processes, agile marketing emphasizes group interactions over rigid approaches and tools, frequent customer collaboration, and rapid responses to change. Kaykas-Wolff shares that "While I worked at Microsoft, I began to experiment. I incorporated agile processes and approaches borrowed from engineering into how we ran marketing programs, first starting with search engine marketing (SEM). It worked very well. Over the past several years a full system of agile marketing has been developed, and it is perfectly suited for Mindjet."[3]

In a nutshell, agile marketing allows small, collaborative teams to work together in short bursts of one to four weeks. The process contains communications tools that allow teams to be articulate, to aggregate large volumes of information and filter it quickly, and to be adaptable. It fosters total transparency across departments. In other words, agile marketing enables mindfulness.

Nearly any project, including print media and advertising, can work within the agile marketing system; however, programs such as content management, lead generation, lead scoring, and new product launches are some of the most promising candidates. These initiatives provide instant feedback, and can be measured and changed on the fly.

In lieu of wholesale campaign changes, Kaykas-Wolff and his team created several small experiments. They started by improving the lead generation process for their top-selling product. "After we assessed the impact of our lead campaigns, we found that 60 percent of our product trials and sales accepted leads were driven by our content marketing strategy. Our agile approach enabled us to drive significant lead growth compared to 2011, resulting in thousands of new marketing qualified leads."[4]

The cost of deploying agile marketing processes was tiny in comparison to the thousands of qualified leads that the new pipeline management campaign generated. Today, Kaykas-Wolff and his agile marketing evangelists host regional meet-ups and a website: www.agilemanifesto.org. Companies such as PriceWaterhouseCoopers and Cisco Systems also successfully use these processes.

NOW THAT YOU KNOW...

The assessment phase gave you enough information to be dangerous; you are now aware of the hand you were dealt. Now it's time to put pen or keyboard to paper and develop your communications and implementation plan. These essential steps will increase your chances of success:

1. *Rehearse how you will communicate your initiative or vision.* Can you explain it with your eyes closed? Does your teenage daughter or son completely understand what you want to accomplish? What is your visceral reaction when you state it out loud? That will tell you how it will land with others. This step is an excellent way to cull out the techno-babble and science-speak from your message. In my experience, technology and life sciences companies are notorious for complicating their messages with these vapid terms.

    Build the habit of following up with your constituents. When you have delegated the task of communicating your vision to others, such as your managers, new groups, or geographic regions, write a follow-up email. This should confirm what you want to see happen and what is expected. To add an extra level of mutual understanding, ask them to repeat back what you have requested.

As you develop your message, consider the orientation of the message. You will notice a subtle, yet cumulative, impact when you are revenue- versus customer-success focused. Just imagine how these small changes can shift people's interpretation of your intentions.

Table 21.1 Internal vs. External Marketing Approaches

Marketing Function	Definition	Internally Focused Question	Externally Focused Question
Branding, Messaging, and Positioning	Your unique identity and story that engage and inspire your communities	How do we present our organization in the best light to the outside world and drive incremental revenue streams?	How do we weave a story about the customer's challenges and the emotional and tangible benefits that they receive (and do not receive) from us?
Go to Market Plan	How someone engages with your product or service, your brand touch points (such as your website), and the options available for them to buy from you.	What sales and marketing channels and strategies will help us reach buyers who will optimize our revenue streams? (e.g., resellers, web portal, direct sales, inside sales)	What go-to market strategy will best align with our customer-centric values, and make it very easy for people to learn, evaluate, and buy from us?
Communications strategy	How your company communicates with customers, analysts, investors, and teams	What methods (online and offline) do we use to create market ubiquity, awareness, and commitment?	How can we remove the clutter from our communications plans and make it easier for individuals to hear us?
Content Strategy	The model used to educate, inform, create market acceptance, and facilitate buying and customer loyalty.	What content will streamline the buying process (such as webinars, web self-service, online forms) and make us more profitable?	What is the profile of our individual buyer(s)? How do they buy from us, or our competitors? How do they like to interact with us? What insights and content can we develop to make their buying experience most satisfying?

Marketing Function	Definition	Internally Focused Question	Externally Focused Question
Roles and Accountabilities	The systems used to ensure customer-facing teams are aligned and rewarded for achieving the top 3–4 company goals.	How do we organize and incent our marketing teams to best serve the sales organization(s)?	How do we organize and incent our marketing teams to inspire, educate, attract, and delight our various (and often unique) customer audiences?
Demand Creation	Systems and processes that expedite and convert qualified leads into sales, both online and offline	How many leads in the pipeline do we need to meet our sales goal?	Where do gaps or delays exist in our buyer experience, and how do we improve them? How do we guide our prospects across every stage of the sales pipeline—even when our sales are strong?
Sales Enablement	The tools, education, and coaching to create consistent, efficient buying and customer experiences	What tools, training, and coaching do our sales teams need to close more business?	What sales behaviors, skills, tools, and activities will we provide and reinforce that reflect our customer-focused culture? What is the best way to transfer that knowledge?
Customer Experience	A roadmap and a clear understanding of the customers' buying journey and ongoing interactions with your company	How do we increase our Net Promoter Score (NPS), customer satisfaction ratings, etc.?	What systems do we need to deploy and align to create a WOW customer experience? How do we engage with our customers to make sure they receive the most value from us? How do we discover unmet customer needs?

Copyright 2014, Lisa Nirell. All rights reserved.

2. *Hire the right people to do the job.* Today, marketing leaders are expected to hire data scientists, content marketing experts, community managers, and online marketing gurus. Many of these positions didn't exist three years ago. It can be a challenge to know what skills and abilities (aka behaviors) you need to fill these nascent positions.

Look in unusual places for data scientists, such as digital agencies, technology firms, and research institutions. Four universities now graduate data analytics experts: University of Virginia, Duke University, Columbia University, and Stanford University. LinkedIn can also help you find companies that hire and develop data scientists, such as IBM, SAS, Cloudera, and Cognos.

If you are searching for a community manager to shepherd customer conversations both online and offline, look outside the traditional walls of the journalism school for talent. Suspend your old definition of "customer community." This role is not about building a LISTSERV, an online forum, or a LinkedIn group. Companies such as Lithium and GetSatisfaction have helped thousands of companies build customer communities that foster two-way collaboration and transparency. The ideal candidate for this position should be a succinct communicator, a savvy social media navigator (not a CRM or sales operations expert), and a compassionate professional. The best community managers stay balanced when a customer complains loudly and publicly. They feel empathy and put themselves in their customers' shoes. That is what makes them effective at storytelling and problem solving.

3. *Write the plan.* Your colleagues are intelligent, but they are not mind readers. Unless we document our plans, our brains have no way of recording and filtering that information. The Reticular Activation System in our brain, or RAS, performs this filing and prioritization function for us.
4. *Create the structure to succeed.* This doesn't refer only to your organization structure. It also includes how you structure your *life*. Do you have your refrigerator stocked with healthy foods to fuel your workweek? Do you turn off your mobile devices during your quiet hours and while you are creating time for reflection? Have you delegated all nonessential tasks to experts, such as housekeepers, landscapers, bookkeepers, and dog walkers? Is your home set up for peaceful sleep? Every creative moment counts. One of my clients once ran a nationally recognized technology consultancy and was still doing her own bookkeeping—until I convinced her that someone could perform this task for a fraction of her billable fee.

5. *Design a balanced marketing program that incorporates past, present, and future thinking.* If you are strictly treated like a marketing drive-through window, you are probably spending over 80 percent of your time either fixing yesterday's chronic problems or making decisions about today's issues and opportunities. That leaves you less than 20 percent of your day to innovate, spot patterns, and think about the future. If you were hired to be a firefighter, and not a fire marshal, rethink your role and your true long-term value at that company. Besides, wearing a fire hose around your neck all day can be exhausting.
6. *Develop courage—and be willing to get fired.* Jeff Hayzlett, former CMO of Kodak, enlisted the help of his IT colleagues and eradicated the old, stodgy employee photos for name badges. Human resources was incensed, even though the name badges had not been updated in years, and reflected poorly on Kodak's *raison d'être*. He didn't care, and he ultimately won the respect of employees.[5]

Mindful revolutionaries like us are not here to hang out on the sidelines. We are here to run the race. These six steps will ensure your mindful marketing programs stay the course.

INNER MARKETING GURU Inquiry #21:

Where can I start a mindful revolution in my organization?

This page intentionally left blank

CHAPTER 22

MINDING THE FUTURE

If you have knowledge, let others light their candles in it.
—Margaret Fuller

In Bangkok, Thailand, in 1955, historians discovered the world's largest gold statue while they were moving a plaster statue to another location in the Wat Traimit temple. During their final attempt to remove the statue from its pedestal, the harnesses and ropes ripped apart. That is when the five-ton statue fell on the ground, and the plaster chipped off to reveal the gorgeous gold statue beneath it. Today, the epic gold Buddha sits on public display. Wikipedia reports that "the time when the gold statue was revealed was very close to the commemoration of the twenty-fifth Buddhist Era (2500 years since Gautama Buddha's passing)...many Buddhists regarded such an occurrence as miraculous." [1]

The golden statue discovery reminds us that, in order to be mindful marketers, we need to make room for our true brilliance to shine. That requires us to remove some of the trappings of our hectic lives. When we remove these superficial plaster molds that we have created to protect us, we discover the brilliance of who we truly are and create room for a new future to emerge.

As I made room for this book to emerge, I turned down unsolicited lunch meetings, "pick your brain" invitations, and fun social outings. This gave me the time to listen more intently to subtle societal and organizational shifts that will impact the future of marketing. Six trends are afoot. Here's the list:

1. *Actionable data, not big data, will win.* Chapter 5 outlined the myriad potential uses of big data for today's modern marketers. The real risk with big data is not the lack of data scientist talent, nor the cost of managing many petabytes worth of information. It is *determining what questions to ask* and what actions you can realistically implement from your insights. Sometimes, that means spending more time in the field with customers, not parsing through reams of analytics.

Chris Brogan opines that "With all that we track online, it's depressing how little of it is used in the service of better customer experiences. I *want* to be known and treated with a familiar experience."[2] He shares a recent occurrence at his favorite Boston hotel: "'Big' data just means that there are mountains of information points that, in the right hands, can make interesting things happen. I think what lots of us need is 'warm' data. What 'warm' means to me is 'data that matters and can help the customer.' Christopher Lynn, who runs a lot of things at the Colonnade Hotel in Boston knew Jacqueline and I were going to a Black Keys concert while staying there one night. We came back to our room to a CD of their music and a nice note. He used warm data to make my perception of the hotel and Chris's dedication to guests that mattered to him very very high indeed." [3]

Finally, never underestimate the power and value of transparent, compassionate team members. Actionable and big data initiatives represent a new way of doing business and interacting with customers. Big data is the customer relationship management and enterprise resource planning of our time. This means that failures are commonplace. Emotions run high when you are introducing change.

Felix Flory, a data scientist contractor with Fusion Technologies, has found that "all of the failures that I've seen are misunderstandings between the scientists and the management teams." He attributes the failures to one of three root causes: setting the wrong expectations, underestimating project complexity, and secrecy. "In most situations, management hears the cool stuff that other companies do in fancy conference presentations. Then they come back and demand the same thing from their employees. The problem is often that the management doesn't have enough time or patience to fully understand the complex requirements in data and personnel. In other cases, management tends to be protective of their department-specific data."[4]

Our brains are not designed around a fixed set of algorithms, and our creative potential is endless. That is why I recommend using big data to augment, not replace, the intuitive gifts and talents of your existing team.

2. *The emergence of the "community economy."* Thanks in part to the democratization of data and round-the-clock access to information, top-down, bureaucratic management is in decline. Customers want to be more engaged in product development. Research proves that they are already in charge of an increasing percentage of the buying process. And they are downright fearless when it comes to sharing their feedback on what it's like to do business with your company. They have turned the traditional capitalist economy on its head.

Seth Kahan, a noted author on change management and the founder of consultancy Visionary Leadership, observes that "the traditional economy is characterized by a desire for consistency and stability. The focus is on making money. This is done by providing a standard experience or service that can be relied upon over and over again to be the same as it was before. You do this by getting really efficient at marketing, production, and delivery...managers are told what to do, and they tell workers what to do. Conversely, the creative economy is characterized by new, exciting offerings, greater customization, and addressing emerging demands with just-in-time solutions. The focus is on *delighting customers profitably*. This is done by getting really good at communicating with customers, engaging them on an ongoing basis, and building relationships that regularly unearth new and better ways of providing value. Communication inside creative organizations happens via two-way conversations at all levels. Everyone is involved in *the quest to discover how to create better offerings*."[5]

Seth shines a light on an emergent pattern in today's workplaces that I am also witnessing. Our mutual interests in this area draw from the work of Steve Denning, the author of a groundbreaking book entitled *The Leader's Guide to Radical Management* and a frequent *Forbes* contributor. These new organizational and decision models will eventually overshadow the traditional economy. I call the new model the "community economy." Fueled by a passion to continuously innovate and improve, it brings together the best qualities of customer engagement, collaboration, rapid project prototyping, horizontal communication, and transparency.

In their personal lives, people naturally seek out these communities to improve their swim technique, build a stronger boat, and learn a new language. Now, today's lifelong learners view innovative communities as an essential piece to also foster their business and professional growth. The architects of those professional communities provide immense—and often irreplaceable—value.

Community managers and departmental change agents are key players in this new economy. Some high technology CEOs whom I have met revere the community manager as the company's "spiritual guide." Part storyteller, trend spotter, analyst, editor, and therapist, they are the alchemists who hold the magic skills needed to engage and inspire.

Top marketers and CEOs understand the intrinsic and financial benefits of maintaining an external focus. While he was VP of Corporate Marketing and Communications for ICF International, Eric Lecky grew his marketing team from 3 to 40 professionals within just a few years. He says that "being externally focused and mindful of your brand is an essential component of any marketing strategy. In our marketing department, we use social media extensively, launching multiple posts a day across different platforms, but almost never to 'market' anything we sell. Instead, we tell stories."

"We talk about employees and interesting things they are doing. We talk about corporate responsibility and how we are helping to make the world a better place. This creates a brand 'alter ego' that counteracts all the traditional self-promotion we do through other channels, and gives customers a very different sense of what the company is all about. I am always more interested in what the social media team is saying than I am in what the next promotional email is about. It's this human interest and culture-creating aspect that really builds brand, and what really matters."[6]

Consider what qualities you will seek in the next person you hire. Do they have a history of working hard for a paycheck, or collaborating and taking risks with others to create breakthroughs in the industry?

3. *It's no longer about you.* I have lost patience with companies that build websites and social platforms that showcase how smart, global, and great they are—and never mention their customers in the process. They write copy in the first person. One professional services firm threw a banner on their website featuring dozens of Fortune 500 company names. You had to dig deep to find this sloppy list. The most prominent page contained some grainy photographs of the executive team, including two who had passed away years ago. I didn't know whether to laugh or feel sorry for them.

   Chris Brogan has a favorite saying that "The Monchu is the Media." *Monchu,* an Okinawan term, means "one family," "extended family," or sometimes "the family we choose," he says. Brogan continues by saying, "'The Monchu is the Media' is my belief that if companies accept that they are all now in the media business, then the next important realization is that the community of people they have the pleasure to serve should be the stars of that story. The more you can write in service of and also about the people who make up the ecosystem, the more you'll have the opportunity to operate with a better chance of success."[7]

   He further explains that "the story alone won't cut it. Community alone gets boring too quickly. Selling without a relationship isn't a marketplace; it's old timey advertising, and works just as badly as it always has. We need all three elements: great content, the tools, and desire to nurture a community who loves that content, and the potential for a community-focused marketplace. That's the model of the UFC (Ultimate Fighting Championship) around mixed martial arts. That's the model of Reebok around Cross Fit."[8]

4. *Agile goes viral.* In the future, the principles behind agile software development will expand beyond research and development and marketing teams. Imagine what would happen if sales and marketing teams were designed around a prospective customer's buying preferences, and they were able to draw appropriate talent from other departments to help streamline the buying experience. Or, what if Voice of the Customer (VoC) teams could launch a feedback system within days versus weeks, tailor their product or service

delivery system dynamically, then report the results within minutes to senior leaders? These steps could reinvigorate an otherwise exhaustive, overwhelming voice of the customer program that typically requires months of planning and launching. The possibilities for agile thinking and operating are endless.

As the workplace loses its hierarchical shackles and becomes more networked, marketers need to allocate a healthy percentage of their earnings to build their skills in seemingly unrelated areas such as agile marketing, predictive analytics, and marketing research—as well as critical thinking, foreign language, philosophy, world history, and foreign affairs. Specialization, coupled with a broad understanding of how the world works, can help marketers rise above a crowded sea of talent. Relying on your employer to invest in your professional development in traditional areas will limit your growth.

5. *Mind-sets get a front row seat on the marketing strategy stage.* I am inspired by the new customer trends in the health and wellness industry. Most people go to spas to relax and unwind. We spend many of our waking hours on physical health and hygiene. Now, mental hygiene is equally, if not more, important. Spafinder Wellness, Inc. claims that providers within the wellness tourism industry, which generated $439B in revenues in 2012, now offer programs that address a person's mind-set.[9]

Professionals who want ongoing support to reinforce their new mindful behaviors can now choose from over 100,000 mindfulness apps online. Wendy Lea, executive chairwoman of Get Satisfaction in San Francisco, California, uses two apps to help her stay focused and centered: calm.com and Focus@Will. No matter what industry you serve or represent, you must factor customer sentiment and behavior change into your market analysis and customer nurturing campaigns, not just traditional demographics (e.g., location, age, job title, and income level). Learning how customers actually feel when they use your product, and how it improves their self-confidence or efficacy, could separate you from how your competitors go to market. Imagine developing an app that connects them to other like-minded individuals, tracks their success, or alerts them to special interest meet-ups in their area.

In 2012, Rubbermaid CMO Richard Davies took a bold step closer toward rapidly integrating customer feedback into every marketing decision. He assumed responsibility for the market research function, doubling the team to 20 people. In a recent *AdAge* interview, he stated that "You lose count of the number of companies who claim the consumer is boss. But the question is do they really make the consumer boss or not? I think by having a strong, independent (research) function you're a hell of a lot closer to doing that."[10]

6. *Unplugged moments matter.* It takes a leap of faith to unplug. Some people whom I have met think of their lives as an "either/or" proposition where they are either relaxed and unplugged, or overworked and hyper-connected. Today, it's about living a "both/and" life. We are human beings, not human doings.

Thousands of studies outlining the benefits of mindfulness, single tasking, and reflection can no longer be ignored. These practices are now mainstream. The *Huffington Post* founder and bestselling author, Arianna Huffington, never brings any mobile devices or computers into her bedroom. During a recent keynote address at a leadership conference in Washington, DC, she proudly announced that she uses an old-fashioned alarm clock and a traditional phone in her bedroom. If her news staff needs to urgently reach her, they have the emergency phone number. Otherwise, the temptation to check emails during waking moments is too strong.

Lecky reports that "Internally, in order to focus and be more 'present' in meetings and work activities, we occasionally have technology-free meetings. It may seem a bit counter intuitive, but shutting off smart phones, email, and even the conference call line creates a much more intimate experience and often spawns a different level of attention, and therefore creativity. I encourage my team to engage this way when possible. It has a certain liberating aspect to be able to block out the world and just focus. We have found this is especially helpful in creative brainstorming sessions—some of our best ideas emerge when we shut off the gadgets." [11]

Whether you are planning a live customer conference or an internal team meeting, create moments to unplug. Build a nap room (a practice which has gained popularity at the *Huffington Post* and Google offices), a place for people to meditate, or practice yoga. Your constituents will be skeptical. Eventually, they will appreciate, if not love, the gesture.

Wikipedia defines nonattachment as a philosophy and a state of mind in which "a person overcomes his or her attachment to desire for things, people or concepts of the world and thus attains a heightened perspective."[12] Nonattachment has been a concept taught by many teachers across multiple faiths ranging from Christianity, Jainism, Taoism, and Buddhism to reduce human suffering.

In the spirit of these timeless mindfulness teachings, I remain nonattached to these 6 predictions. I really don't care how many people reading these insights agree with me. I simply encourage you to pursue the ones that make sense and discard the ones that do not. Somewhere within these insights lies your golden statue, your Inner Marketing Guru.

INNER MARKETING GURU Inquiry #22:

As I remove layers of distractions from my life, what insights and market trends are emerging?

ABOUT LISA NIRELL

Lisa Nirell speaks frequently at annual conferences and executive retreats.

As a marketing leadership advisor, growth strategist, and award-winning author, Lisa brings provocative insights and practical marketing wisdom to her clients. Companies such as Adobe, Infor, Oracle, GenRe, and Bozzuto hire her to help them dramatically accelerate growth and build customer mindshare. She contributes regularly to *Fast Company*, *The Huffington Post*, and the CMO Council. Guy Kawasaki praised her first book, *EnergizeGrowth NOW: The Marketing Guide to a Wealthy Company*, saying "by applying these time-tested planning guides, you will have changed the world for the better."

In her workshops and speeches, Lisa awakens your teams and leaders to the realities of today's customer-driven marketplace, and how to harness those opportunities. You see results in the form of breakthrough ideas, improved decision-making, higher profits, and faster time to execution.

An avid yogini, philosophy student, and meditation practitioner, Lisa resides near Washington, DC with her husband, Magnus, and their two mindful cats.

Download your bonus videos, and additional resources at www.themindfulmarketer.com/bonus.

To learn more or book Lisa Nirell for your upcoming event, visit www.energizegrowth.com or contact_us@energizegrowth.com.

This page intentionally left blank

NOTES

1 WHY CMOS ARE FACING EXTINCTION

1. Gartner Group "By 2017 the CMO Will Spend More on IT than the CEO," January 3, 2012 webinar, http://my.gartner.com/portal/server.pt?open=512&objID=202&mode=2&PageID=5553&resId=1871515 (accessed September 6, 2013).
2. Nick Eades, interview with author, September 16. 2013.
3. John A. Byrne, "She's Doing an Elite MBA for Under $1,000," LinkedIn, http://www.linkedin.com/today/post/articlc/20140117183101-17970806--she-s-doing-an-elite-mba-for-under-1-000, January 17, 2014 (accessed February 21, 2014).
4. David Houle and Jonathan Fleece, "Why One-Third of Hospitals Will Close by 2020," KevinMD.com, March 14, 2012, http://www.kevinmd.com/blog/2012/03/onethird-hospitals-close-2020.html (accessed February 21, 2014).
5. Dan Markovitz, interview with author, October 23, 2013.
6. Russell Parsons, "Marketers Should Be Responsible for Sales," *Marketing Week*, April 6, 2012, http://www.marketingweek.co.uk/news/marketers-should-be-responsible-for-sales/4001064.article?goback=%2Egmp_51822%2Egde_51822_member_100645153%2Egmp_51822%2Egde_51822_member_106782475#%21 (accessed September 6, 2013).
7. Andrew McAfee and Erik Brynjolfsson, "Big Data: The Management Revolution," *Harvard Business Review*, October 2012, page 64.

2 THE DARK SIDE OF DATA DEMOCRACY

1. Brad Meltzer, *The Inner Circle* (New York: Grand Central Publishing/Hatchette Group, 2011).
2. Malala Yousafzai, speech to the United Nations Youth Assembly on Malala Day, New York, July 12, 2013, http://ibnlive.in.com/news/full-text-of-malala-yousafzais-speech-at-united-nations/406812-2.html (accessed October 8, 2013).
3. Adrian C. Ott, *The 24 Hour Customer: New Rules for Winning in a Time-Starved, Always Connected Economy* (New York: Harper Collins, 2010), page 6.
4. Ibid., page 22.

5. Natalie Zmuda, Rupal Parekh, "Keeping Time: Why CMO Time Has Doubled," *AdAge*, May 6, 2013, http://adage.com/article/cmo-interviews/keeping-time-cmo-tenure-doubled/241294/ (accessed September 12, 2013).
6. Joe Payne, interview with author, June 3, 2013.

3 GOING DIM: CAN YOU SEE (OR HEAR) ME NOW?

1. "In Praise of Laziness," *The Economist*, (August 17, 2013), page 58.
2. Alan Weiss, interview with author, September 12, 2013.
3. Elizabeth Corcoran, "Dell Moves Outsourced Jobs Back to U.S. Shores," *Forbes*, April 24, 2004, http://www.nbcnews.com/id/4853511/ns/business-forbes_com/t/dell-moves-outsourced-jobs-back-us-shores/#.Ui-IST_9zbw (accessed September 13, 2013).
4. Tony Schwartz, "The Power of Stepping Back," *Dealbook New York Times*, http://dealbook.nytimes.com/2013/09/06/the-power-of-stepping-back/?_r=1& (accessed September 13. 2013).

4 RETURN ON MARKETING INVESTMENTS: A FLIGHT RISK?

1. "CMOs' Top Priority Is Figuring out How Best to Engage with Customers," Korn Ferry, June 28, 2013, http://www.kornferry.com/press/675/ (accessed February 21, 2014).
2. Jim Lenskold, "Experimenting Your Way to More Effective Marketing," Lenskold Group, December 2009, http://www.lenskold.com/content/articles/lenskold_dec09.html (accessed November 14, 2014.)
3. Ron Wince, "ROI Revealed for Customer Experience Strategy: Peppers and Rogers Group Strategy Speaks, April 22, 2013, http://www.peppersandrogersgroup.com/blog/2013/04/roi-revealed-for-customer-expe.html (accessed November 14, 2013).
4. Daniel Kehrer, "Why ROI Is Often Wrong for Measuring Market Impact," *Forbes*, July 9, 2013, http://www.forbes.com/sites/forbesinsights/2013/07/09/why-roi-is-often-wrong-for-measuring-marketing-impact/ (accessed November 14, 2013).
5. Ibid.
6. Dominique Hanssens, interview with author, September 25, 2013.

5 BIG DATA OR BIG DISAPPOINTMENT?

1. Jeremy Campbell, *Grammatical Man: Information, Entropy, Language and Life* (New York: Simon & Schuster, 1982). Used with permission.
2. Andrew McAfee and Erik Brynjolfsson, "Big Data: The Management Revolution," *Harvard Business Review*, October 2012, http://hbr.org/2012/10/big-data-the-management-revolution/ar/1 (accessed September 6, 2013).

3. Copyright 2013 Caroulsel30, used with permission.
4. Pradeep Kumar, "Case Study: How redBus Uses BigQuery to Master Big Data," *Google BigQuery*, https://developers.google.com/bigquery/case-studies/redbus (accessed February 25, 2014).
5. Derrick Harris, "LinkedIn University Pages Are a Case Study in Building Big Data Apps the Right Way," *GIGAOM*, http://gigaom.com/2013/08/28/linkedin-university-pages-are-a-case-study-in-building-big-data-apps-the-right-way/ (accessed February 25, 2014).
6. Dan Riskin, MD, "Natural Language Processing: Putting Big Data to Work to Drive Efficiencies and Improve Patient Outcomes," *HISTalk*, http://histalk2.com/2013/08/26/readers-write-natural-language-processing-putting-big-data-to-work-to-drive-efficiencies-and-improve-patient-outcomes/ (accessed February 25, 2014).
7. Tyler Douglas, interview with author, September 3, 2013. See also http://www.visioncritical.com/client-stories/nascar (accessed September 6, 2013).
8. Andrew McAfee and Erik Brynjolfsson, "Big Data: The Management Revolution," *Harvard Business Review*, October 2012, http://hbr.org/2012/10/big-data-the-management-revolution (accessed September 6, 2013).
9. Infochimps, "CIOs and Big Data: What Your IT Team Wants You to Know," 2013, http://bigdata.infochimps.com/Portals/174427/docs/infochimps%20report%20-%20cios%20and%20big%20data%20report.pdf (accessed September 6, 2013).
10. Alexis C. Madrigal, "We Have the Whole History of the Web Wrong," *The Atlantic*, October 12, 2012, http://www.theatlantic.com/technology/archive/2012/10/dark-social-we-have-the-whole-history-of-the-web-wrong/263523/ (accessed September 6, 2013).
11. *our understanding, per Laurie Harting, no citation required for works older than 75 years, correct?*
12. Jill Richards, interview with author, August 20, 2013.
13. Arianna Huffington, Wisdom 2.0 Conference, San Francisco, CA, February 2013.

6 MARKETING AND SALES: A HARD LANDING

1. Gil Fronsdal, "Equanimity," Insight Meditation Center, http://www.insight-meditationcenter.org/books-articles/articles/equanimity/, May 29, 2004 (accessed December 4, 2013).
2. Brian Kardon, interview with author, October 8, 2013.
3. Charles Gold, interview with author, October 7 2013.
4. Mike Troiano, interview with author, March 28, 2013
5. Michael Ni, interview with author, October 9, 2013.
6. Marit Fratelli, "2013 State of the Sales Rep Report: Content Strategies Drive Sales Effectivenes" Brainshark Ideas Blog, November 8, 2013, http://www.brainshark.com/ideas-blog/2013/November/2013-state-of-the-sales-rep-report.aspx (accessed October 8, 2013)

7. Charles Gold, "The Content Factory," April 30, 2012, http://cgoldmarketing.com/2012/04/30/the-content-factory/ (accessed October 7, 2013)
8. "2013 B2B Content Marketing Benchmarks, Budgets, and Trends," MarketingProfs, October 24, 2012, http://www.marketingprofs.com/charts/2012/9184/2013-b2b-content-marketing-benchmarks-budgets-and-trends (accessed October 9, 2013)
9. http://www.articulate.com/products/daily-demo.php Articulate Corporation website (accessed October 20, 2013).
10. The ON24 Webinar Benchmark Index: An Industry First, ON24, http://www.on24.com/press_releases/the-on24-webinar-benchmark-index-an-industry-first/ (accessed February 25, 2014).
11. Jill Konrath, "5 Important Questions for Your First Meeting," Jill's Jottings: Fresh Sales Strategies, January 2013, http://www.jillkonrath.com/sales-blog/bid/112356/5-Important-Questions-for-Your-First-Meeting?utm_source=twitter&utm_medium=social&utm_content=2182772 (accessed October 11, 2013)

7 MULTITASKING MASH-UPS AND MISHAPS

1. Teresa M. Amabile, Jennifer S. Mueller, William B. Simpson, Constance N. Hadley, Steven J. Kramer, Lee Fleming, "Time Pressure and Creativity in Organizations: A Longitudinal Field Study," Harvard Business School Division of Research, 2002, page 22. Used with permission. http://www.hbs.edu/faculty/Pages/item.aspx?num=11879
2. Steve Lohr, "Slow Down, Brave Multitasker, and Don't Read This in Traffic," *The New York Times*, March 25, 2007, http://www.nytimes.com/2007/03/25/business/25multi.html?pagewanted=all&_r=0 (accessed December 4, 2013).
3. Paul E. Dux, Jason Ivanoff, Christopher L. Asplund, and Rene Marois, "Isolation of a Central Bottleneck of Information Processing with Time-resolved fMRI," US National Library of Medicine/National Institute of Health, http://www.ncbi.nlm.nih.gov/pmc/articles/PMC2527865/ (accessed December 4, 2013).
4. Dennis E. Clayson, Debra A. Haley, "An Introduction to Multitasking and Texting: Prevalence and Impact on Grades and GPA in Marketing Classes," *Journal of Marketing Education*, December 6, 2012, http://jmd.sagepub.com/content/35/1/26.abstract December 6, 2012, published online before print. (accessed December 4, 2013).
5. Bill Chappell, "Stanford Professor Who Sounded Alert on Multitasking Has Died," KPBS Public Radio, November 7. 2013, http://www.kpbs.org/news/2013/nov/07/stanford-professor-who-sounded-alert-on/ (accessed December 4, 2013).
6. Gloria Mark, Victor M. Gonzales, Justin Harris, "No Task Left Behind? Examining the Nature of Fragmented Work," University of California, Irvine, 2005, http://www.ics.uci.edu/~gmark/CHI2005.pdf (accessed December 4, 2013).
7. Ibid.

8. Teresa M. Amabile, Jennifer S. Mueller, William B. Simpson, Constance N. Hadley, Steven J. Kramer, Lee Fleming, "Time Pressure and Creativity in Organizations: A Longitudinal Field Study," Harvard Business School Division of Research, 2002.
9. Brian Scudamore, interview with author, October 28 2013.
10. Kristin Piombrino, "Infographic: The Biggest Reason Employees Waste Time at Work," ragan.com: news and ideas for communicators, October 29, 2013, http://www.ragan.com/Main/Articles/47482.aspx# (accessed December 4, 2013).
11. The Effects of Multitasking on Organizations, Realization White Paper, Realization, August 26, 2013, http://www.realization.com/pdf/Effects_of_Multitasking_on_Organizations.pdf (accessed December 16, 2013).
12. Ibid.

8 FIND YOUR *INNER MARKETING GURU* TO MAKE BETTER DECISIONS

1. Danna Faulds, "Walk Slowly," *Go In and In: Poems from the Heart of Yoga* (Greenville, VA: Peaceable Kingdom Books, 2002).
2. Omega Institute, "Mindfulness in the Modern World: An Interview with Jon Kabat Zinn," *Huffington Post*, October 7, 2012, http://www.huffingtonpost.com/omega-institute-for-holistic-studies/jon-kabat-zinn_b_1936784.html (accessed December 12, 2013)
3. Ibid.
4. Piyadassi Thera, "The Seven Factors of Enlightenment," http://www.accesstoinsight.org/lib/authors/piyadassi/wheel001.html (accessed December 12, 2013).
5. Ibid.
6. Allie Gray Freeland, "Four Lessons Marketers Can Learn from Yoga," Marketing Profs, http://www.mpdailyfix.com/four-lessons-marketers-can-learn-from-yoga/ (accessed December 12, 2013).
7. David Gelles, "The Mind Business," *FT Magazine*, http://www.ft.com/intl/cms/s/2/d9cb7940-ebea-11e1-985a-00144feab49a.html#axzz2nHkQtOPP (accessed December 12, 2013).
8. David Gelles, "The Mind Business," *Financial Times Magazine*, http://www.ft.com/intl/cms/s/2/d9cb7940-ebea-11e1-985a-00144feab49a.html#axzz2nHkQtOPP (accessed December 12, 2013).

9 WESTERN MINDFULNESS: A BRIEF JOURNEY

1. From the book *The Power of Now*, Copyright © 1997 by Eckhart Tolle. Reprinted with permission of New World Library, Novato, CA. www.newworldlibrary.com.
2. Maharishi Mahesh Yogi, interview with Merv Griffith, 1975, http://www.youtube.com/watch?v=wGVKJ5O5mEw&feature=c4-overview-vl&list=PL3E4AA0011DCDAAB0 (accessed December 12, 2013).

3. Lisa Nirell, *EnergizeGrowth NOW* (Hoboken, NJ: John Wiley & Sons, 2009), page 12.
4. Alan Weiss, "The Power of Language," Million Dollar Consulting® Mindset, October 2011, http://summitconsulting.com/million-dollar-consulting-mindset-newsletter/2011-10.php (accessed February 19, 2014).
5. Keith Sawyer, "Why Ron Johnson's Apple Magic Failed J.C. Penney," *MarketWatch*, http://www.marketwatch.com/story/why-ron-johnsons-apple-magic-failed-jc-penney-2013-04-10 (accessed February 26, 2014).
6. Christopher S. Penn, interview with author, November 27, 2013.

10   FIVE TIMELESS QUALITIES OF MINDFUL MARKETERS

1. Daryl Conner, "The Need to Care for Character," *The Cultivating Character Series*, Conner Partners, January 22, 2013, http://www.connerpartners.com/practicing-our-craft/the-need-to-care-for-character (accessed December 16, 2013).
2. Ibid.
3. Daryl Conner, "Reflections on Character and Presence," Conner Partners, 2013, http://www.connerpartners.com/wp-content/uploads/Reflections-on-Character-and-Presence1.pdf (accessed December 16, 2013).
4. Daryl Conner, "How Does Our Presence Reflect Our Character," *The Cultivating Character Series*, Conner Partners, January 3, 2013, http://www.connerpartners.com/practicing-our-craft/how-does-our-presence-reflect-our-character#sthash.i90ahnP0.dpuf (accessed December 16, 2013).
5. Deborah Sandella, "Living Fully Lights On," *Science of Mind*, July, 2013, http://www.scienceofmind.com/pdf/mag/2013/july/som_july2013_content.pdf (accessed December 16, 2013).
6. Cathy and Gary Hawk, *Get Clarity©: The Lights-On Guide to Manifesting Success in Life and Work*, (Get Clarity Press, 2012), page 113. Used with permission
7. Brian Solis, *Leading Transformation and Captivating Communities* (Change This Manifestos, 2011) http://changethis.com/manifesto/show/89.02.LeadingTransformation (accessed December 16, 2013).
8. Marianne Williamson, *A Return to Love* (New York: Harper Collins, 2012).

11   PERSONAL ENERGY MANAGEMENT

1. Melissa Korn, "The State of the American Workplace Is...Meh," *At Work Blog: Wall Street Journal*, June 11, 2013, http://blogs.wsj.com/atwork/2013/06/11/the-state-of-the-american-workplace-is-meh/ (accessed January 8, 2014).
2. Ibid.
3. "Think Yourself Well," *The Economist*, December 8 2012, page 80.
4. Ibid.
5. Carla M. Thompson, RN BscN, "The Map of Consciousness—Hawkins Scale," Stankof's Universal Law Press, January 19, 2012, http://www.stankovuniversallaw

.com/2012/01/the-map-of-consciousness-hawkins-scale/ (accessed January 8, 2014).
6. The Personality Development Blog, http://personality-development.org/theories-personality-development/david-hawkins Personality-Development.org features a succinct description of Dr. David Hawkins' levels of consciousness. The website refers to itself as "an online resource for useful information relating to theories of personality development, developmental psychology, educational theory, giftedness, high ability studies, peak performance, and all related fields of psychology and psychoanalysis." Sheldon Kreger is the primary contributor.
7. David Hawkins, *Power VS. Force* (Carlsbad, CA: Hay House Press, 2002), page 238.
8. Ibid. page 96.
9. Cathy and Gary Hawk, *Get Clarity©: The Lights-On Guide to Manifesting Success in Life and Work*, (Get Clarity Press, 2012), page 14.
10. Ibid.
11. "Our Reason for Being," Patagonia website, http://www.patagonia.com/us/patagonia.go?assctid=2047 (accessed February 21, 2014).
12. Cathy and Gary Hawk, *Get Clarity©: The Lights-On Guide to Manifesting Success in Life and Work*, (Get Clarity Press, 2012), page 16.
13. Sherry Turkle, "Communication, Wisdom, and True Connection in the Digital Age," Wisdom 2.0 Conference 2013, http://www.youtube.com/watch?v=MZ6qYIt3Fdw (accessed January 8, 2014).
14. Cathy and Gary Hawk, *Get Clarity©: The Lights-On Guide to Manifesting Success in Life and Work*, (Get Clarity Press, 2012), page 17.
15. Ibid. page 18.
16. Tony Schwartz, "Keep Calm and Carry On," The Energy Project blog, http://theenergyproject.com/blog/keep-calm-and-carry (accessed January 8, 2014).

12 THE POWER OF PRESENT MOMENT LANGUAGE

1. Chip Conley, "Emotional Equations," *Big Think*, June 25, 2012, http://bigthink.com/videos/emotional-equations-2 (accessed January 9, 2014).
2. Drake Baer, "Leadership Now: How to Create Your Own Luck," *Fast Company*, November 27, 2013, http://www.fastcompany.com/3022297/leadership-now/how-to-create-your-own-luck (accessed January 9, 2014).
3. Alan Weiss, "Persuasion Pyramid," Society for the Advancement of Consulting conference, October 9, 2013. Used with permission.
4. Douglas Van Praet, "Feeling Your Consumer: What Marketers are Missing about Making Emotional Connections," *Fast Company CoCreate*, November 25, 2013, http://www.fastcocreate.com/3022151/compassion-vs-competition-what-marketers-are-missing-about-making-emotional-connections?partner=newsletter (accessed January 9, 2014).
5. Steve Yastrow, *We: The Ideal Customer Relationship* (New York: SelectBooks, 2007), page 78.

6. Ibid., page 79.
7. "Why Does Gratitude Feel So Good?" *7 Gen Blog*, November 18, 2013, http://www.seventhgeneration.com/learn/blog/why-does-gratitude-feel-so-good (accessed January 9, 2014).
8. Cathy and Gary Hawk, *Get Clarity©: The Lights-On Guide to Manifesting Success in Life and Work*, (Get Clarity Press, 2012). Also *SHIFT, A Guidebook to Above-the-Line, Positive Thinking* (Get Clarity Press, 2013). www.getclarity.com
9. Jason Lake, interview with author, November 27, 2013.
10. John Morris, interview with author, September 26, 2013.
11. Bryant Jaquez, interview with author, November 27, 2013.

13   MINDFUL PLANNING AND DECISION-MAKING

1. John Chaffee, *The Thinker's Way* (New York: Little, Brown & Company, 1998), pages 38–39.
2. Ibid., page 41.
3. Ibid., page 41.
4. Ibid., page 42.
5. Carol Stratford, interview with author, December 4, 2013.

14   DESIGNING WITH INTENTION

1. Luanne Bradley, "Tracking Sustainability in Architecture," *Dwell*, February 4, 2014, http://www.dwell.com/post/article/tracking-sustainability-architecture (accessed February 4, 2014).
2. Ibid.
3. Ibid.
4. Ibid.
5. Ibid.
6. Ibid.
7. Christopher S. Penn, interview with author, December 8, 2013.
8. Paul Sheng, interview with author, December 10, 2013.
9. Ibid.
10. "10 Big Companies That Promote Employee Meditation," OnlineMBA, February 1, 2012, http://www.onlinemba.com/blog/10-big-companies-that-promote-employee-meditation/ (accessed February 4, 2014).
11. Paul Sheng, interview with author, December 10, 2013.
12. Ibid.
13. Christopher S. Penn, interview with author, December 8, 2013.
14. Leah Zerbe, "Houseplants Can Make You Happy," *Rodale News*, October 13, 2008, http://www.rodalenews.com/plants-and-happiness (accessed February 4, 2014).
15. Tatiana Pagés, interview with author, December 12, 2013.

16. Laura Vanderkam, "10 Quick Tips to Create a Home Office You'll Actually Want to Work In," *Fast Company*, December 12, 2013, http://www.fastcompany.com/3023303/work-smart/10-quick-tips-to-bring-your-home-office-to-another-level?partner=newsletter (accessed February 4, 2014).
17. Image copyright © Enlightened; used with permission.
18. Tushar Dave, interview with author, December 13, 2013.
19. Christopher S. Penn, interview with author, December 8, 2013
20. Barbara Messing, interview with author, December 9, 2013.

15 PEER GROUPS: HOW SHIFTS *REALLY* HAPPEN

1. John Naisbitt, *Megatrends: Ten New Directions Transforming Our Lives* (New York: Warner Books, 1982).
2. Douglas Van Praet, interview with author, December 9, 2013.
3. Ibid.
4. Ibid.
5. Bruce Peters, interview with author, December 17, 2013.
6. Ibid.
7. Ibid.
8. Alison Whitmire, interview with author, December 16, 2013.
9. Cathy and Gary Hawk, *Get Clarity©: The Lights-On Guide to Manifesting Success in Life and Work*, (Get Clarity Press, 2012). Also *SHIFT, A Guidebook to Above-the-Line, Positive Thinking* (Get Clarity Press, 2013). www.getclarity.com
10. Alison Whitmire, interview with author, December 16, 2013.
11. Ibid.
12. Bruce Peters, interview with author, December 17, 2013.
13. Simon Angove, interview with author, September 13, 2010.
14. Bob Arciniaga, interview with author, August 5, 2010.
15. Colin Gounden, interview with author, August 6, 2010.
16. Marnie Ochs-Raleigh, interview with author, January 2, 2014.
17. Luc Vezina, interview with author, August 14, 2010.
18. Ian Knox, interview with author, November 29, 2010.

16 WHAT THE CEO WANTS THE CMO TO KNOW

1. Buddha, Dhammapada, verse 80 http://www.tipitaka.net/tipitaka/dhp/verseload.php?verse=080.
2. Dan Pink, *To Sell Is Human: The Surprising Truth About Moving Others* (New York: Riverhead Books, 2012), page 21.
3. Lattice Engines, "Grow Revenue with Big Data," Marketing and Sales Knowledge Hub, March 11, 2013, http://www.lattice-engines.com/resources/ebooks/grow-revenue-with-big-data?source=mprofsguestpost (accessed January 20, 2014).
4. McKinsey & Company, used with permission

5. Joe Dunsmore, interview with author, January 3, 2014.
6. Christopher Penn, SHIFT Communications, interview with author, December 8, 2013.

17 CFO-SPEAK: MINDFUL MARKETING BY THE NUMBERS

1. Gary Patterson, interview with author, January 14, 2014.
2. "Five Key Enterprise Technology Trends for 2014," CFO Innovation Asia, December 19, 2013, http://www.cfoinnovation.com/content/five-key-enterprise-technology-trends-2014?page=0%2C1 (accessed January 31, 2014).
3. Don Clarke, interview with author, January 7, 2014.
4. Larry Freed, *Innovating Analytics: Word of Mouth Index: How the Next Generation of Net Promoter Can Increase Sales and Drive Business Results* (Hoboken, NJ: John Wiley & Sons, 2013), page 207.
5. Ibid., page 208.
6. Ibid., page 212.
7. Ibid., page 208.
8. Ibid., page 98.
9. Jonathan Gordon, Jean-Hugues Monier, and Phil Ogren, "Why Can't We Be Friends? Five Steps to Better Relations between CFOs and CMOs," *Insights & Publications*, McKinsey & Company, December 2013, http://www.mckinsey.com/Insights/Corporate_Finance/Why_cant_we_be_friends_Five_steps_to_better_relations_between_CFOs_and_CMOs?cid=other-eml-alt-mip-mck-oth-1312 (accessed January 28, 2014).
10. Val Wright, interview with author, January 9, 2014
11. Ibid.
12. Gary Patterson, "Know Your Numbers for Greater Profits," *Million Dollar Blind Spots: 20/20 Vision for Financial Growth* (Issaquah, WA: AudioInk Publishing, 2012)

18 THE CMO AND THE CIO: CROSSING THE RAGING RIVER

1. David Gerrold, "Zen and the Art of Whatever," 1997, http://www.taoism.net/articles/zenart.htm (accessed February 8, 2014).
2. Jerry Grochow, interview with author, January 14, 2014.
3. Ibid.
4. "The CMO and CIO Must Accelerate on Their Path to Better Collaboration," Forrester Research, October 31, 2013.
5. Ibid.
6. Ibid.
7. Wayne McKinnon, interview with author, January 15, 2014
8. Patrick Gray, "Challenges Facing the CIO in 2014," ZDNet, November 13, 2013, http://www.zdnet.com/challenges-facing-the-cio-in-2014-7000022666/ (accessed February 8, 2014).

9. Ibid.
10. "The CMO and CIO Must Accelerate on Their Path to Better Collaboration," Forrester Research, October 31, 2013
11. Karen Quintos, interview with author, October 16, 2013.
12. "The Role of the CIO in 2014," *BusinessTech*, January 5, 2014, http://businesstech.co.za/news/it-services/50570/the-role-of-the-cio-in-2014/ (accessed February 8, 2014).
13. Ibid.
14. Kim S. Nash, "State of the CIO 2014: The Great Schism," CIO, January 1, 2014, http://www.cio.com/article/744601/State_of_the_CIO_2014_The_Great_Schism (accessed February 8, 2014).
15. Copyright © 2013, Wayne McKinnon, "Why Service Providers and Customers Remain Susceptible to a Value Gap," The McKinnon Group, 2013, www.themckinnongroup.com. Used with permission.
16. Wayne McKinnon, interview with author, January 16, 2014.
17. Karen Quintos, interview with author, October 16, 2013.
18. Ibid.
19. Ibid.

19   SALES AND MARKETING: RETHINKING THE SYSTEM

1. Donald T. Phillips, *Martin Luther King on Leadership* (New York: Warner Books, 1998).
2. Tim Riesterer, interview with author, January 6, 2014.
3. Michael Ni, interview with author, October 19, 2013.
4. Tim Hill, interview with author, January 15, 2014
5. Andy Zimmerman, interview with author, November 5, 2013
6. Greg Jorgensen, interview with author, January 25, 2014
7. Ibid.
8. Greg Jorgensen, interview with author, January 19, 2014
9. Ibid.

20   LOOKING INSIDE TO WORK OUTSIDE

1. MacFarquhar, Larissa, "The Better Boss: How Marshall Goldsmith Reforms Executives," *The New Yorker*, 2002, http://www.marshallgoldsmithlibrary.com/cim/articles_print.php?aid=73 (accessed February 11, 2014).
2. Jan-Patrick Schmitz, interview with author, January 16, 2014.
3. Ibid.
4. Ibid.
5. Ibid.
6. Ibid.
7. Ibid.
8. Ibid.
9. Steve Cody, interview with author, January 28, 2014.

10. Ibid.
11. Ibid.
12. Ibid.
13. Lisa Evans, 3 Ways Improv Can Improve Your Career, *Fast Company*, http://www.fastcompany.com/3025570/3-ways-improv-can-improve-your-career?partner=newsletter), January 31, 2014 (accessed February 11, 2014).
14. The Standish Group, The CHAOS Manifesto 2013: Think Big, Act Small, 2013, http://versionone.com/assets/img/files/ChaosManifesto2013.pdf (accessed February 11, 2013).
15. David Fields, interview with author, August 26, 2013.
16. Ibid.
17. Ibid.
18. Sandy Katz, interview with author, January 29, 2014.
19. Ibid.
20. Ibid.
21. Chris Pick, interview with author, January 29, 2014.
22. Ibid.
23. Ibid.
24. Ibid.

21   STARTING THE REVOLUTION

1. Jascha Kaykas-Wolff, interview with author, January 17, 2013
2. Ibid.
3. Ibid.
4. Ibid.
5. Jeffrey Hayzlett keynote presentation, Eloqua Experience Conference 2012, Orlando Florida, November 7, 2012.

22   MINDING THE FUTURE

1. "Golden Buddha (Statue), Wikipedia, http://en.wikipedia.org/wiki/Golden_Buddha_%28statue%29 (accessed February 18, 2014).
2. Chris Brogan, interview with author, February 3, 2014.
3. Chris Brogan, "Trends for 2014," Human Business Works, http://www.humanbusinessworks.com, (accessed December 15, 2013).
4. Felix Flory, interview with author, February 11, 2014.
5. Seth Kahan, "The Creative Economy Is Here," *Monday Morning Mojo*, Visionary Leadership, February 9, 2014, (accessed February 10, 2014) http://www.visionaryleadership.com/site/monday-morning-mojo-archive.php.
6. Eric Lecky, interview with author, February 7, 2014.
7. Chris Brogan, interview with author, February 3, 2014.
8. Chris Brogan, "What the Heck Is a Monchu?" *Owner Magazine*, August 6, 2013, http://ownermag.com/what-the-heck-is-a-monchu/?inf_contact_key

=89a7aad0cfaf7e4bde4a3417a9bbcc2884cac03d714f509f83e13b8c9657a853 (accessed February 18, 2014).
9. "2014 Global Spa & Wellness Trends Forecast Webinar," Spafinder Wellness, January 14, 2014, https://www.youtube.com/watch?v=1IjFx1xSt2A&feature=share&utm_source=TrendsWebinarThankyou011414&utm_medium=email&utm_campaign=14012 (accessed February 18, 2014).
10. Jack Neff, "Newell Rubbermaid Shakes Up CMO Model By Putting Research in Charge," *AdAge*, February 5, 2014 http://adage.com/article/cmo-strategy/newell-rubbermaid-shakes-cmo-model/291377/?utm_source=cmo_strategy&utm_medium=newsletter&utm_campaign=adage&ttl=1392228101 (accessed February 18, 2014).
11. Eric Lecky, interview with author, February 7, 2014.
12. "Detachment (philosophy)," Wikipedia, http://en.wikipedia.org/wiki/Detachment_(philosophy) (accessed February 18, 2014).

This page intentionally left blank

INDEX

24-Hour Customer, The (Ott), 13, 20

accountabilities, 45, 135, 170, 180, 191
accountability standards, 28, 95, 130
Actifio, 44–5
AdAge, 201
affective empathy, 98, 126–7
aggregation, 84, 182–3, 185
agility, defined, 138
aliveness, 82, 176–9, 185
Allen Morris Company, 119
Amabile, Teresa, 51, 55
Amazon, 5, 33, 152
AMC network, 46
American Express Global Customer Service Barometer, 28
Angove, Simon, 131
APE: Author, Publisher, and Entrepreneur (Kawasaki and Welch), 5
Apple, 75, 91, 97, 118
Apptio, 183
Arciniaga, Bob, 132
Articulate (e-learning site), 14, 47
articulate marketing, 95, 103, 153
articulateness, 83–4, 176, 180–81, 185, 188
Ascendant Consortium, 180
Ashton-Tate, 145
Asiana Airlines, 25
Association to Advance Collegiate Schools of Business (AACSB), 6
attractor fields, 88–9

Baer, Drake, 96–7
Barnes & Noble, 5
Basex, 53

Beaudoin, Cathy, 152
Benioff, Marc, 27
Bezos, Jeff, 96–7, 152
Biomorphic Biosphere, 116
Blockbuster, 97
bluebirds, 43, 170
BMC Software, 172
book publishing, 5
Bradley, Luanne, 116
Brainshark, 45, 170
Breaking Bad, 46
breathwork sessions, 71–2, 77
brick-and-mortar retailers, 5–6
Brogan, Chris, 196, 199
Brynjolfsson, Erik, 35
Bucke, Richard Maurice, 37
Buddha Sutra, 1
Buddhism, 41, 63–4, 71–2, 75, 105, 177, 195, 202
budgets, 3–4, 8, 26–9, 66, 99, 101, 137, 141, 147, 150–1, 157–60, 180
buyer experience, 44, 191
Byrne, John, 6

Campbell, Jeremy, 31
candor, 161, 163–4
Carousel30, 32
Center for Disease Control, 182
Chaffee, John, 106–7
chanting, 71
Check-In Process, 66, 101–2, 129, 192
Chopra, Deepak, 71
Chouinard, Yvon, 91
Cisco, 23, 183, 189
Clarity International, 82–3, 90, 101
  See also Hawk, Cathy and Gary

Clarke, Don, 147
Clayson, Dennis, 53
"Closing the Gap" model, 162
Coca-Cola, 16
Cody, Steven, 178
cognitive empathy, 97–8, 126
collaboration, 45, 54, 100, 132–4, 146, 151–2, 159, 161, 169, 181–2, 187–8, 192, 198
Compaq, 31, 39, 41
compassion, 16, 23, 62, 82, 119, 161–3, 192, 196
concentration, defined, 64
Conley, Chip, 96
Conner, Daryl, 20, 79–81
content sources, 46
cortisol, 65
Cradle To Cradle model, 115
critical thinking, 10, 105–7, 111–13, 200
Cross Fit, 199
CrossWorlds Software, 172–3
customer experience, 23, 32, 44, 150, 152, 156, 159–61, 168, 172, 191, 196
Customer Experience movement, 28
customer focus, 138, 161
Customer Relationship Management (CRM), 29, 43, 101, 138

"Dark Triad" personality vortex, 98
data democratization
  affect on customers, 13–15
  affect on internal stakeholders, 15–17
  overview, 11–13
Dave, Tushar, 120
Davies, Richard, 201
decision-making, collaborative, 8, 28, 32, 35, 38, 66, 81, 83, 100, 105–14, 167
Dell, 23, 159, 162–3
Digital Equipment (DEC), 145
digital intrusion movement (DIM)
  indicators, 20–3
  overview, 19–20
DiLoreto, Larry, 170
Distant Energy System, 92

Douglas, Tyler, 34
Dunsmore, Joe, 142

Eades, Nick, 3
e-learning/online education, 6, 14
Eloqua, 7, 15–16, 26, 162
Emerson, Ralph Waldo, 61, 95, 185
Emotional Equations (Conley), 96
empathy
  affective, 98, 126–7
  cognitive, 97–8, 126
Enchantment (Kawasaki), 5
Energy Project, The (Schwartz), 24
enterprise resource planning (ERP), 158, 196
equanimity, 41, 48, 62, 65–6
Evans, Lisa, 179
Executive's Guide to Consultants, The (Fields), 180

Facebook, 4, 13, 52, 125, 160
FastCompany, 93, 96, 179
Faulds, Danna, 59
Fenn, Jackie, 35
Fields, David, 180–1
Flatow, Ira, 53
Fleece, Jonathan, 6
Flory, Felix, 196
ForeSee, 148
Forrester, Jay, 166
Forrester Groundswell Award, 34
Forrester Research, 157–8
FoundHere.com, 117–18
Franklin, Benjamin, 145
Frederickson, Barbara, 88
Freed, Larry, 148–50
Freedland, Allie Gray, 65
Fronsdal, Gil, 41

gaming, 6–7
"gaming the system," 148
Gandhi, Mahatma, 87
Gap, 152
Gartner Group, 3, 35
Gasper, Kevin, 152
GE Solutions, 7

Gelles, David, 65
General Mills, 65
GetSatisfaction, 192
Gilligan, Vince, 46
Glover, Toni, 12, 56, 63, 156, 179
go-arounds, 26
Godin, Seth, 5
GOJO Industries, 182
Gold, Charles, 44, 47
Goldsmith, Marshall, 175
Google, 7, 64–5, 96–7, 118, 201
Gounden, Colin, 132
Gray, John, 41
Gray, Patrick, 158
Great Recession, 27, 96
Green Machine, 116
Green Mountain Coffee, 65
green movement, 116, 118–19
Greencard Creative, 119
Greene, Alan, 182
greenfield leads, 171
Grochow, Jerry, 156
Gupta, Sanjeev, 57

Hanssens, Dominique, 29–30
happiness, defined, 64
Hawk, Cathy and Gary, 82, 90–3, 101, 129
  See also Clarity International
Hawkins, David, 88–90
Hayzlett, Jeffrey, 110, 193
health care, 6
Heskett, John, 73
Hill, Tim, 169–70
Hoar, Joseph, 23, 82
hospitals, 6
Houle, David, 6
Huffington, Arianna, 38, 201
Huffington Post, 38, 64, 201
Human Energy System, 90–1
Hype Cycle for Emerging Technologies, 35

iAcquire, 65
IBM, 7, 41, 173, 192
Ingels, Bjarke, 116
Inner Marketing Guru (IMG), 10, 62–3, 66

Innovating Analytics (Freed), 148
innovation, 22, 27–8, 51, 55, 79, 93, 116–17, 130, 134, 149–50, 156, 160, 163, 183
intentionality, 96–7, 100, 107, 117
International Data Corporation (IDC), 35, 159–60
International Financial Reporting Standards (IFRS), 147
iPad, 97
  See also Apple
Isetan, 177

J. Walter Thompson, 178
Jaquez, Bryant, 103
JC Penney, 5, 75
Jobs, Steve, 91
Johnson, Ron, 75
Joie de Vivre Hotels, 96
Jois, Sri K. Pattabhi, 72
Jones, Wes, 116
Jones, Will, 145
Jorgensen, Greg, 172–3

Kabat-Zinn, Jon, 61–2
Karaboutis, Adriana, 159, 162–3
Kardon, Brian, 43
Katz, Sandy, 182–3
Kawasaki, Guy, 5, 203
Kaykas-Wolff, Jascha, 188–9
Kehrer, Daniel, 30
key performance indicators (KPIs), 109, 141–2
Knox, Ian, 134
Kodak, 110, 193
Kok, Bethany, 88
Konrath, Jill, 48
Korn/Ferry, 26
Kotter, John, 73
KPBS, 53
Kravitz, Judith, 71

Lake, Jason, 102
language, 16, 21, 23, 33, 42, 66, 70, 75–7, 90–1, 93, 95–103, 139–41
Lao Tzu, 79

Lawrence, D. H., 175
Lecky, Eric, 198, 201
LEED certification, 116
Lenskold, Jim, 27
LinkedIn, 4, 6, 13, 22–3, 33, 52, 125, 192
LISTSERV, 192
Lithium, 192
Lynn, Christopher, 196

Machiavellianism, 98
Macy's, 5, 75
Madrigal, Alexis C., 36
Magee, Fred, 160
Maharishi Mahesh Yogi, 71
Mark, Gloria, 54
marketing language meter, 100
Markovitz, Dan, 6
Marois, Rene, 53
Massive Open Online Courses (MOOCs), 6
McAfee, Andrew, 35
McDonough, William, 115–17
McKinnon, Wayne, 158, 161–2
McKinsey, 118, 151
media exposure, 92
meditation, 23, 57, 62, 64–5, 70–2, 76, 88, 118, 201
Meier, Richard, 115
Meltzer, Brad, 11
Meng Tzu, 3
Messing, Barbara, 122
Microsoft, 188
MicroStrategy, 16
Mind & Life Institute, 70
mindful marketers, qualities of
  acceptance, 79–80
  aggregation, 84–5
  aliveness, 82–3
  articulateness, 83–4
mindfulness, Western
  attitudes, 74
  beliefs, 74
  breathworksessions, 71–2
  chanting, 71
  decisions, 75
  defined, 70
  language, 75–6
  memories, 74–5
  overview, 79
  presence, 80–2
  Qigong, 72
  silent meditation, 70–1
  Tai Chi, 73
  values, 73–4
  why it works, 76
  yoga, 72–3
Mindfulness Based Stress Reduction (MBSR), 61
Mindjet, 188
Miraval Resort and Spa, 111–13
Moed, Ed, 178
Monchu, 199
Montblanc, 176–7
Morris, John, 103
MultiMate International, 145
multitasking
  counterproductive nature of, 20
  overview, 51–3
  reasons for reducing, 53–5
  ways to reduce, 55–7
MyHabit, 152

Naisbitt, John, 125
NASCAR, 33–5
Nash, Kim, 160
Nass, Clifford, 53–4
National Consumer League, 182
Near Field, 91
Net Promoter Score, 28, 140, 191
Netflix, 33, 97
New Health Age, The (Houle and Fleece), 6
Ni, Michael, 45, 167
Nielsen, Steven, 116
Nielsen research, 177
Noble Creative, 103
Northrup, Christiane, 71

Ochs-Raleigh, Marnie, 133
Office Space, 122
OfficeMax, 176

OnTarget, 41
Oracle, 7, 15, 26, 41
Orthomolecular Psychiatry (Hawkins), 88
Ott, Adrian, 13, 20

Pagés, Tatiana, 119
Patagonia, 91
Patterson, Gary, 146, 152
Pauling, Linus, 88
Payne, Joe, 15–16, 143
Penn, Christopher, 76, 117–18, 121
Peppercomm, 178
Performance Accelerant Model (PAM), 108
Perry, Jenny, 152
Perry, William, 106
persona, 80
personal field, 90–1
persuasion, defined, 138
persuasion pyramid, 97
Peters, Bruce, 128–9
Pick, Chris, 183
Pickard, Laurie, 6
pilot error, 26
pilotage principles, 161–4
Polizzi, Nicole "Snooki," 12
Powell, Colin, 82
Power vs. Force (Hawkins), 88–9
presence, 80–2, 85
Progress Principle, The (Amabile), 51
psychotherapy, 126
Purell, 182

Qigong, defined, 72
Quintos, Karen, 159, 162–3

Rackham, Neil, 7–8
reality TV, 12
Reebok, 199
Reichheld, Frederick, 28
Remote Field, 92
responsibility, lines of, 3–4
Reticular Activation System (RAS), 91, 108, 192
return on investment (ROI), 7, 15–16, 27, 134

Richards, Jill, 38
Riesterer, Tim, 166–7
Rubbermaid, 201
RueLaLa, 152

Salesforce.com, 27, 162
Sandberg, Sheryl, 20
Sandella, Deborah, 82
SAP Community Network (SCN), 103
Schmitz, Jan-Patrick, 176–7
Schwartz, Tony, 24, 93
Science Friday, 53
Science of Mind, 82
Scudamore, Brian, 55
service-level agreements (SLAs), 170–1
Seventh Generation, 15
Sheng, Paul, 117–18
SHIFT Communications, 76, 117–18, 121
Siebel Systems, 41
Small, Glen, 116, 118
smartphones, 6, 32, 52
social media
    CMOs and, 135, 139–40, 142, 150
    customer relations and, 125, 192
    data democratization and, 15–16
    design and, 116
    experts, 8, 12, 22
    marketing and, 47, 84, 198
    mindfulness and, 75–6
    NASCAR and, 34–5
    Near Field and, 92
    product development and, 32, 34
    relevance and, 8
    tensions and, 4
    Three Horizons Model and, 142
    transparency and, 4
Solis, Brian, 84
Standish Group, 180
Stanford University, 53, 70, 192
Staples, 176
Stratford, Carol, 111, 114
Stuart, Spencer, 15

Tai Chi, 73
Target, 5, 65, 75

Taxi Magic, 6
technology business management (TBM), 183
Terracotta Technologies, 38
Thera, Piyadassi, 64
Thompson, Alana "Honey Boo Boo," 12
Thompson, Carla, 89
Thoreau, Henry David, 115
Three Horizons Model, 141–2
Toffler, Alvin, 116
Tolle, Eckhart, 69
Tom's Shoes, 15
traditional industries, 5–7
transparency, 4, 12, 103, 143, 149, 167, 187–8, 192, 196, 198
TripAdvisor, 122
Troiano, Mike, 44
true nature, 63, 80, 103
Turkle, Sherry, 91
Twitter, 13, 16, 84, 139, 141

Uber, 6
UFC (Ultimate Fighting Championship), 199
Unconscious Branding (Van Praet), 98, 126–7
unplugged moments, 23, 62–4, 73, 91, 201
US government shutdown, 96

Van Praet, Douglas, 98, 126–7
Vanderkam, Laura, 120
Vezina, Luc, 133

Wang, 145
Warrior, Padmasree, 23
"waterfall" development process, 188
We: The Ideal Customer Relationship (Yastrow), 99
Weiner, Jeff, 23
Weiss, Alan, 21, 75, 97–8
Welch, Shawn, 5
Whitmire, Alison, 128–9
Williamson, Marianne, 85
wisdom, 38–9, 62, 79, 182
Wright, Val, 152

Yastrow, Steve, 99
yoga
    Ashtanga, 72–3
    equanimity and, 65
    Hatha, 72
    overview, 72
Yousafzai, Malala, 12

Zappos, 81, 84, 152
ZDNet, 158
Zerbe, Leah, 119
Zimmerman, Andy, 170
Zinn, Jon Kabat, 61–2, 71

GPSR Compliance
The European Union's (EU) General Product Safety Regulation (GPSR) is a set of rules that requires consumer products to be safe and our obligations to ensure this.

If you have any concerns about our products, you can contact us on

ProductSafety@springernature.com

In case Publisher is established outside the EU, the EU authorized representative is:

Springer Nature Customer Service Center GmbH
Europaplatz 3
69115 Heidelberg, Germany

www.ingramcontent.com/pod-product-compliance
Lightning Source LLC
LaVergne TN
LVHW020329260326
834688LV00037B/934